HARASSMENT IN THE WORKPLACE

by
Margaret C. Jasper

Oceana's Legal Almanac Series:
Law for the Layperson

2002
Oceana Publications, Inc.
Dobbs Ferry, New York

Library of Congress Control Number: 2002112334

ISBN: 0-379-11370-8

Oceana's Legal Almanac Series: Law for the Layperson
ISSN 1075-7376

To My Husband Chris

Your love and support
are my motivation and inspiration

-and-

In memory of my son, Jimmy

Table of Contents

CHAPTER 3:
THE NATURE OF WORKPLACE HARASSMENT

CHAPTER 4:
SEXUAL HARASSMENT

CHAPTER 8:
PROTECTING YOUR RIGHTS

APPENDICES

ABOUT THE AUTHOR

MARGARET C. JASPER is an attorney engaged in the general practice of law in South Salem, New York, concentrating in the areas of personal injury and entertainment law. Ms. Jasper holds a Juris Doctor degree from Pace University School of Law, White Plains, New York, is a member of the New York and Connecticut bars, and is certified to practice before the United States District Courts for the Southern and Eastern Districts of New York, the United States Court of Appeals for the Second Circuit, and the United States Supreme Court.

Ms. Jasper has been appointed to the panel of arbitrators of the American Arbitration Association and the law guardian panel for the Family Court of the State of New York, is a member of the Association of Trial Lawyers of America, and is a New York State licensed real estate broker and member of the Westchester County Board of Realtors, operating as Jasper Real Estate, in South Salem, New York. Margaret Jasper maintains a website at http://members.aol.com/JasperLaw.

Ms. Jasper is the author and general editor of the following legal almanacs: Juvenile Justice and Children's Law; Marriage and Divorce; Estate Planning; The Law of Contracts; The Law of Dispute Resolution; Law for the Small Business Owner; The Law of Personal Injury; Real Estate Law for the Homeowner and Broker; Everyday Legal Forms; Dictionary of Selected Legal Terms; The Law of Medical Malpractice; The Law of Product Liability; The Law of No-Fault Insurance; The Law of Immigration; The Law of Libel and Slander; The Law of Buying and Selling; Elder Law; The Right to Die; AIDS Law; The Law of Obscenity and Pornography; The Law of Child Custody; The Law of Debt Collection; Consumer Rights Law; Bankruptcy Law for the Individual Debtor; Victim's Rights Law; Animal Rights Law; Workers' Compensation Law; Employee Rights in the Workplace; Probate Law; Environmental Law; Labor Law; The Americans with Disabilities Act; The Law of Capital Punishment; Education Law; The Law of Violence Against Women; Landlord-Tenant

Law; Insurance Law; Religion and the Law; Commercial Law; Motor Vehicle Law; Social Security Law; The Law of Drunk Driving; The Law of Speech and the First Amendment; Employment Discrimination Under Title VII; Hospital Liability Law; Home Mortgage Law Primer; Copyright Law; Patent Law; Trademark Law; Special Education Law; The Law of Attachment and Garnishment; Banks and their Customers; Credit Cards and the Law; Identity Theft and How To Protect Yourself; Welfare: Your Rights and the Law; Individual Bankruptcy and Restructuring; Harassment in the Workplace; and Health Care and Your Rights.

INTRODUCTION

According to the EEOC, harassment continues to be a serious problem in American workplaces. The number of harassment charges filed with the EEOC and state fair employment practices agencies has risen significantly in recent years.

Employees should be permitted to work in an environment free from conduct that is offensive, humiliating or abusive, and laws have been enacted to protect workers from unlawful workplace harassment. Workplace harassment has generally been defined as unwelcomed or unsolicited speech or conduct based upon an individual's race, sex, creed, religion, national origin, age, color, or handicapping condition, that creates a hostile work environment.

Workplace harassment also encompasses situations where a sexual "quid pro quo" environment exists—i.e., where employment decisions are based on an employee's submission or rejection of unwelcome sexual advances. Retaliation against employees who report incidents of workplace harassment is also prohibited.

This almanac discusses the various situations that give rise to workplace harassment complaints, which requires both an objective and subjective analysis of the particular behaviors. Some actions, on their face, clearly fall under illegal workplace harassment. However, there are instances where it is more difficult to draw the line between behaviors that may be unacceptable to some individuals, but not to the degree of illegality. What one individual finds repugnant may not be perceived as particularly offensive to another. Specific actions which have been held to constitute unlawful workplace harassment are examined in order to assist the reader in understanding the types of behaviors which may give rise to a such a charge.

This almanac also explores the various remedies available to victims of workplace harassment to address this serious problem, including the more stringent guidelines established by the Equal Employment Opportunity Commission under the 1991 amendment to Title VII of the Civil Rights Act of 1964.

This almanac also sets forth information concerning employer liability for workplace harassment, and recommendations employers may follow to effectively prevent and correct harassment. This would include the establishment and distribution of a written anti-harassment policy, describing the prohibited behaviors and setting forth clear guidelines for handling complaints and addressing violations.

The Appendix provides resource directories, applicable statutes, and other pertinent information and data. The Glossary contains definitions of many of the terms used throughout the almanac.

CHAPTER 1:
OVERVIEW OF ANTI-HARASSMENT LAWS

GOVERNING LAW

Workplace harassment is prohibited under both federal and state laws. Title VII of the Civil Rights Act (Title VII) prohibits harassment of an employee based on race, color, sex, religion, or national origin. The Americans with Disabilities Act (ADA) prohibits harassment based on disability, and the Age Discrimination in Employment Act (ADEA) prohibits harassment of employees who are 40 or older on the basis of age. All of the anti-discrimination statutes enforced by the EEOC prohibit retaliation for complaining of discrimination or participating in complaint proceedings.

Title VII and the ADA cover all private employers that employ 15 or more employees, as well as state and local governments, educational institutions, private and public employment agencies, labor organizations, and joint labor management committees controlling apprenticeship and training. The ADEA covers all private employers with 20 or more employees, as well as state and local governments, employment agencies and labor organizations.

All employees, including part-time and temporary workers, are counted for purposes of determining whether an employer has a sufficient number of employees. An employee is someone with whom the employer has an employment relationship. The existence of an employment relationship is most easily shown by a person's appearance on the employer's payroll, but this alone does not necessarily answer the question. Independent contractors are not counted as employees. If you are unsure whether your business is covered, or whether an individual who works for you is covered, you may wish to consult with an attorney.

As further discussed in Chapter 2, the Equal Employment Opportunity Commission (EEOC) enforces the anti-discrimination laws against private employers, and the Department of Justice (DOJ) enforces these laws against state and local governments. Nevertheless, individuals who believe they are victims of discrimination, including unlawful workplace harassment, must initially file their charge with the EEOC. The EEOC is responsible for investigating individual charges of discrimination.

Employers are required to post notices to all employees advising them of their rights under the laws that the EEOC enforces, as well as their right to be free from retaliation for bringing charges of discrimination, cooperating in an investigation, or testifying in connection with such charges. These notices are also required to be accessible to persons with visual or other disabilities that affect reading.

TITLE VII OF THE CIVIL RIGHTS ACT OF 1964

Title VII of the Civil Rights Act of 1964 is the principal piece of federal legislation that prohibits employment discrimination, including workplace harassment, based on race, color, national origin, sex, and religion. Discrimination is prohibited in any aspect of employment, including recruitment, hiring, promotion, benefits, training, job duties, and termination. Title VII prohibits not only intentional discrimination, but also outlaws practices that have the "effect" of discriminating against individuals on these bases.

Selected provisions of Title VII of the Civil Rights Act of 1964 are set forth at Appendix 1 of this almanac.

THE CIVIL RIGHTS ACT OF 1991

The Civil Rights Act of 1991 amended Title VII to strengthen and assist in the enforcement of Title VII provisions, and clarify provisions regarding disparate impact actions. The Act also provides for compensatory and punitive damages in cases of intentional employment discrimination, as well as provisions for obtaining attorneys' fees.

The Civil Rights Act of 1991 is set forth at Appendix 2 of this Almanac.

THE AMERICANS WITH DISABILITIES ACT OF 1990

Title I of the Americans with Disabilities Act of 1990 (ADA) prohibits discrimination in employment against a qualified individual with a disability because of the disability. Harassment of an individual because of his or her disability is also unlawful under the Act. In addition, it also is unlawful under the Act for an employer to take retaliatory action against any individual for opposing employment practices made unlawful by the ADA or for filing a discrimination charge or for testifying or assisting or participating in an investigation, proceeding, or hearing under the ADA.

THE AGE DISCRIMINATION IN EMPLOYMENT ACT OF 1967

The Age Discrimination in Employment Act of 1967 (ADEA) protects individuals who are 40 years of age or older from discrimination and workplace harassment. Harassment of an individual because of his or her age is also prohibited under the Act, as well as retaliation against someone who complains about a discriminatory practice, files a charge, or assists in an investigation of discrimination in any way. Congress has designated the EEOC as the federal agency responsible for investigating individual charges of discrimination under the ADEA.

STATE AND LOCAL LAWS PROHIBITING DISCRIMINATION AND HARASSMENT

Many states and municipalities have also enacted prohibitions against discrimination and workplace harassment. In addition, such laws may offer even greater protections against discrimination and harassment based on sexual orientation, status as a parent, marital status and political affiliation. Thus, the reader is advised to check the law of his or her jurisdiction when researching workplace harassment issues.

LAWS PROHIBITING DISCRIMINATION IN FEDERAL EMPLOYMENT

There are additional federal laws which are not enforced by the EEOC, that prohibit discrimination of, and retaliation against, federal employees and applicants.

The Civil Service Reform Act of 1978

The Civil Service Reform Act of 1978 (CSRA) contains a number of prohibitions, known as prohibited personnel practices, which are designed to promote overall fairness in federal employment. The CSRA prohibits federal employees who have authority to take, direct others to take, recommend or approve any personnel action from discriminating against applicants and employees on the bases of race, color, sex, religion, national origin, age, disability, marital status or political affiliation and from discriminating against an applicant or employee on the basis of conduct which does not adversely affect the performance of the applicant or employee.

The Office of Personnel Management (OPM) has interpreted the prohibition of discrimination based on conduct to include discrimination based on sexual orientation. The CSRA defines ten other prohibited personnel practices in the federal government, all of which fall under the jurisdiction of the Office of Special Counsel (OSC) and the Merit Systems Protection Board (MSPB). The CSRA also prohibits retaliation against federal employees or applicants for whistle-blowing, or for exercising an appeal, complaint, or grievance right.

Executive Order 11478

Executive Order 11478, signed in 1969, mandated that all Federal agencies establish equal opportunity offices to address discrimination in employment in the federal sector based on race, color, religion, sex, national origin, handicap,and age. The Order further appointed the Equal Employment Opportunity Commission to implement the policy and further its objectives.

Executive Order 13087

Executive Order 13087, signed in 1998, amended Executive Order 11478 to provide a uniform policy for the federal government to prohibit discrimination based on sexual orientation.

Executive Order 13087 did not create any new rights, however it did set the stage for positive and constructive action by all units of the federal government to make certain that the workplace is one free from harassment and discrimination.

The text of Executive Orders 11478 and 13087 is set forth at Appendix 3.

Executive Order 13152

Executive Order 13152, signed in 2000, also amended Executive Order 11478 to provide for a uniform policy for the federal government to prohibit discrimination based on an individual's status as a parent. Executive Order 13152 states that "status as a parent" refers to the status of an individual who, with respect to an individual who is under the age of 18 or who is 18 or older but is incapable of self-care because of a physical or mental disability, is: (1) a biological parent; (2) an adoptive parent; (3) a foster parent; (4) a stepparent; (5) a custodian of a legal ward; (6) in loco parentis over such an individual; or (7) actively seeking legal custody or adoption of such an individual. The Order authorized the Office of Personnel Management (OPM) to develop guidance on the provisions of this Order.

CHAPTER 2:
THE EQUAL EMPLOYMENT OPPORTUNITY COMMISSION AND RELATED AGENCIES

THE EQUAL EMPLOYMENT OPPORTUNITY COMMISSION

The United States Equal Employment Opportunity Commission (EEOC) is an independent federal agency established by Congress in 1964 to enforce Title VII of the Civil Rights Act of 1964. The EEOC is composed of five Commissioners and a General Counsel appointed by the President and confirmed by the Senate. Commissioners are appointed for five-year staggered terms. The General Counsel's term is four years. The President designates a Chairman and a Vice-Chairman. The Chairman is the chief executive officer. The Commissioners have the authority to establish equal employment policy and to approve litigation. The General Counsel is responsible for conducting litigation.

The EEOC's mission is to promote equal opportunity in employment through administrative and judicial enforcement of the federal laws which prohibit discrimination, including workplace harassment. The EEOC also offers broad-based educational outreach and technical assistance programs, and provides a range of informational materials and assistance to individuals and entities with rights and responsibilities under EEOC-enforced laws. Most materials and assistance are provided to the public at no cost, including posters advising employees of their equal employment opportunity rights, and pamphlets, manuals, fact sheets, and enforcement guidance on laws enforced by the EEOC.

The EEOC is also responsible for promulgating and issuing regulations and other guidance materials to assist in interpreting the laws it enforces, and for administering the federal sector employment discrimination program. The EEOC also provides funding and support to state and local fair employment practices agencies (FEPAs).

A directory of U.S. Equal Employment Opportunity Commission offices is set forth at Appendix 4.

The EEOC Administrative Enforcement Program

The EEOC's administrative enforcement program handles approximately 75,000 charges filed annually. Under the EEOC charge processing system, charges are prioritized into one of three categories for purposes of investigation and resource allocation:

1. Category A—Category A charges are priority charges to which offices devote principal investigative and settlement efforts.

2. Category B—Category B charges are those where there appears to be some merit but more investigation is needed before a decision is made on handling the charge.

3. Category C—Category C charges include non-jurisdictional, self-defeating, or unsupported charges which are immediately closed.

The EEOC Mediation Program

The EEOC encourages settlement of charges at all stages of the investigatory and enforcement process. In that connection, the EEOC has launched a mediation-based alternative dispute resolution (ADR) program.

A directory of EEOC Mediation offices is set forth at Appendix 5.

As more fully discussed in Chapter 7 of this almanac, the mediation program is administered by neutral mediators who promote informed, voluntary, and confidential participation and deliberation by all parties.

STATE AND LOCAL FAIR EMPLOYMENT PRACTICES AGENCIES

As set forth below, many states and localities have enacted anti-discrimination laws, and formed agencies responsible for enforcing those laws. The EEOC refers to these agencies as Fair Employment Practices Agencies (FEPAs). Each charge of discrimination that is covered by both an EEOC-enforced statute and the FEPA's law is dual-filed under both laws, regardless of which agency receives it. These dual-filed charges are typically investigated by only one agency. This way, employers avoid two investigations of the same matter, but the legal rights of the charging parties are still preserved under both laws.

In some cases, where a charge is dual-filed with a FEPA and the EEOC, the EEOC may decide that it does not have jurisdiction or does not believe federal law is violated. However, that is not the end of the complaint. Some state and local laws have longer charge filing periods than the EEOC, cover more employers than those covered by the federal anti-discrimination laws, or provide greater protections than federal law, such as laws prohibiting marital status or sexual orientation harassment. In those cases, the FEPA may continue to investigate the charge.

A directory of state equal employment offices is set forth at Appendix 6.

THE MERIT SYSTEMS PROTECTION BOARD

Along with the Office of Special Counsel (OSC), the Merit Systems Protection Board (MSPB) enforces the prohibitions against federal employment discrimination codified in the Civil Service Reform Act (CSRA), as amended, which is discussed more fully in Chapter 1 of this almanac.

The MSPB is an independent body that hears, among other things: (1) appeals from certain federal agency personnel actions; and (2) cases brought by the Office of Special Counsel (OSC) involving alleged prohibited personnel practices.

Contact for the MSPB is as follows:

Merit Systems Protection Board
1120 Vermont Avenue N.W.
Washington, DC 20419
Telephone Number: 202-653-7200
Toll-Free Number: 1-800-209-8960
Website: http://www.mspb.gov

THE OFFICE OF SPECIAL COUNSEL

The Office of Special Counsel (OSC) is an independent investigative and prosecutorial agency within the Executive Branch of the Federal government that receives and investigates complaints alleging prohibited personnel practices, including those involving discrimination based upon sexual orientation. The OSC receives and investigates allegations from applicants, employees and former employees of prohibited personnel practices, and investigates allegations to determine whether there are reasonable grounds to believe that the agency has committed a prohibited personnel practice or will do so.

The OSC may also request the MSPB to stop personnel actions from taking place while it is investigating whether they were taken as a result of a prohibited personnel practice. These prohibited personnel practices include discrimination based on conduct which does not adversely affect either the employee's own job performance or the performance of others. The OSC may also petition the MSPB for corrective action to provide a remedy for the employee; and seek disciplinary action by the

MSPB against the individuals who committed a prohibited personnel practice.

The OSC attempts to achieve favorable results for employees without litigation by achieving settlements of complaints prior to the initiation of any formal appeal to MSPB. Pending an investigation, the OSC any act as an intermediary between the employee and the agency to resolve issues, and may seek an informal stay of a personnel action to prevent imminent harm when it has reasonable grounds to believe the employee has been subjected to a prohibited personnel practice.

Contact for the OSC is as follows:

Office of the Special Counsel
1730 M Street, NW, Suite 300
Washington, D.C. 20036-4505
Complaints Examining Unit Number: 202-653-7188
Toll-Free Number: 1-800-872-9855
Public Information Number: 202-653-7984
Website: http://www.osc.gov

THE OFFICE OF SPECIAL COUNSEL FOR IMMIGRATION RELATED UNFAIR EMPLOYMENT PRACTICES

The Office of the Special Counsel for Immigration Related Unfair Employment Practices (OSC) is part of the Civil Rights Division of the U.S. Department of Justice. OSC's national origin jurisdiction covers small employers with more than three but less than 15 employees. National origin charges made against larger employers are referred to the EEOC or the appropriate state agency.

The OSC protects work-authorized individuals, including both immigrants and U.S. citizens, from employment discrimination based on national origin and citizenship or immigration status. The OSC investigates four kinds of unfair employment practices: citizenship status and national origin discrimination with respect to hiring, firing, or referral or recruiting for a fee, unfair employment verification procedures, e.g., document abuse, and retaliation.

OSC contact information for employers and employees is as follows:

Office of Special Counsel for Immigration Related Unfair Employment Practices
P.O. Box 27728
Washington, D.C. 20038-7728
Toll-Free Automated Employer Hotline: 1-800-255-8155
Toll-Free Number: 1-800-255-7688
TDD for the Hearing Impaired: 1-800-237-2515
Website: http://www.usdoj.gov/crt/osc

CHAPTER 3:
THE NATURE OF WORKPLACE HARASSMENT

UNLAWFUL WORKPLACE HARASSMENT DEFINED

All employees are guaranteed the right to work in an environment free from unlawful workplace harassment. Workplace harassment is a form of discrimination which violates federal and state law. Title VII is the primary piece of federal legislation prohibiting employment discrimination, including workplace harassment.

Workplace harassment is generally defined as unwelcomed or unsolicited speech or conduct based upon race, creed, sex, religion, national origin, age, color, or disability. Persons who fall into one of the foregoing categories are considered to be in a "protected class" under workplace harassment law.

Additional federal, state, and local laws prohibiting workplace harassment may cover other bases for employment discrimination, including harassment based on sexual orientation, marital status, political affiliation, etc. Thus, the reader is advised to check the law of his or her own jurisdiction in this regard.

Although the most common workplace harassment complaints involve sexual harassment, unlawful workplace harassment is not limited to sexual harassment complaints. The Equal Employment Opportunity Commission (EEOC) has taken the position that the same basic anti-harassment standards apply to all types of prohibited harassment of protected classes, whether it involves race, creed, sex, religion, national origin, age, color, or disability.

The law does not prohibit actions which constitute simple teasing, offhand comments, or isolated incidents that are not serious. The conduct must be sufficiently frequent or severe to create a "hostile work environment" or, in the case of a supervisor, result in a "tangible employment action," such as hiring, firing, promotion, or demotion. Workplace harassment may also involve "quid pro quo" sexual harassment, where the conditions of a victim's employment are subjected to their willingness to provide sexual favors to a person in a position of power over them. A harassment charge may also be based on "retaliation" for an employee's opposition to discrimination, or participation in an investigation or complaint proceedings.

EXAMPLES OF UNLAWFUL WORKPLACE HARASSMENT

Some examples of behaviors which have been considered unlawful workplace harassment are:

1. Avoiding or excluding someone due to race, age, sex, religion, etc.;

2. Using verbal insults or degrading remarks;

3. Making unwelcome jokes about disability, race, sex , etc..

4. Offensive physical contact or coercive behavior which is intended to be derogatory or intimidating, such as unwanted touching, patting, or lewd physical conduct;

5. Making insulting or threatening gestures;

6. Making unjustified and unnecessary comments about a person's work or capacity for work;

7. Making phone calls, letters or messages of any kind which are threatening, abusive or offensive;

8. Persistent following or stalking within or to and from the workplace;

9. Dismissive treatment or material expressing prejudice or stereotypical statements;

10. The continual exclusion of a person or group from normal conversations, work assignments, work related social activities and networks in the workplace;

11. Sexual or racial banter, crude conversation, innuendo and offensive jokes; and discriminatory use of management/supervisory power;

12. A supervisor-promised promotion if employee agrees to a sexual relationship; and

13. Displaying or circulating pictures, posters, graffiti or written materials which are offensive or obscene.

HOSTILE WORK ENVIRONMENT

A hostile work environment is one that both a reasonable person would find hostile or abusive and one that the particular person who is the object of the harassment perceives to be hostile or abusive. Harassment which may constitute a hostile environment is anything that creates fear, intimidates, ostracizes, psychologically or physically threatens, embarrasses, ridicules, or in some other way unreasonably overburdens or precludes an employee from reasonably performing his/her work.

Other circumstances, including the frequency of the alleged harassing conduct, its severity, whether it is physically threatening or humiliating, and whether it unreasonably interferes with an employee's work performance must be considered.

A hostile work environment would exist when members of a protected class are subjected to comments, innuendos, insults, jokes, slurs, and other demeaning conduct, which is related to their membership in the protected class, and which creates an intimidating and offensive work atmosphere.

In a sexual harassment claim, a hostile work environment is one in which the victim, male or female, is subjected to unwelcome and severe or pervasive repeated sexual comments, jokes, innuendoes, touching, or other conduct of a sexual nature which creates an intimidating or offensive place for employees to work. A hostile work environment would also be one in which there is the display of sexually oriented materials in the workplace.

Employers and supervisors have a legal duty to prevent employees from being harassed. In order to make sure the workplace is free from unlawful harassment, the employer and/or supervisor should carefully monitor the workplace for potential problems and make the necessary inquires if a problem is perceived. All complaints should be investigated immediately and taken seriously. Make sure the internal complaint procedures are followed and report the matter to others who should be involved in resolving such problems, such as the human resources representative. Although a thorough investigation should take place, the confidentiality and privacy rights of all parties should be maintained to the degree possible.

QUID PRO QUO SEXUAL HARASSMENT

Quid pro quo sexual harassment generally consists of unwelcome sexual advances, requests for sexual favors, or other verbal or physical conduct carried out by someone who is in a position of power over the victim. Quid pro quo sexual harassment would exist when: (1) submission to such conduct is made either explicitly or implicitly a term or condition of an individual's employment, or (2) submission to or rejection of such conduct by an individual is used as the basis for employment decisions affecting such individual.

UNLAWFUL HARASSMENT OF PROTECTED CLASSES

In order for the illegal conduct to be considered workplace harassment, it must be related in some way to the employee's membership in one of the protected classes. If some adverse employment action is being taken against the employee, such as the denial of a promotion, because it involves their sex or race, this would constitute discrimination.

However, if the employee is being denied the promotion because the supervisor doesn't like the employee, without any evident problems related to their race, sex, creed, religion, national origin, age, color or disability, it would not be considered workplace harassment, although it may be prohibited on some other basis.

HARASSMENT ON THE BASIS OF RACE OR COLOR

The protected class of "race" refers to a local geographic or global human population distinguished as a more or less distinct group by genetically transmitted immutable characteristics, such as skin color, hair texture and certain facial features; and any group of people united or classified together on the basis of common history, nationality, or geographical distribution. All people are allowed to claim one or more races and are, therefore, readily covered under this category. The EEOC counts people as White, Black, Asian/Pacific Islander, Other & Hispanic. However, Hispanic is not considered a race but an ethnic designation because there are Hispanic people of African, European, Indian & mixed heritages. The protected class of "color" refers to people of varying complexions and shades of skin.

Harassment on the basis of race and/or color violates Title VII of the Civil Rights Act. Ethnic slurs, so-called racial jokes, offensive or derogatory comments, or other verbal or physical conduct based on an individual's race or color constitutes unlawful harassment if the conduct creates an intimidating, hostile, or offensive working environment, or if it interferes with the individual's work performance.

HARASSMENT ON THE BASIS OF RELIGION OR CREED

The protected class of "religion" refers to all aspects of religious observance, practice and belief which include moral or ethical beliefs as to what is right and wrong which are sincerely held with the strength of traditional religious views. This would include Buddhists, Catholics, Jews, Protestants, Muslims, Taoists, Atheists, etc.

The protected class of "creed" refers to any statement or system of belief, principles or opinions. Creed is very similar to religion but is not always a religion. This may include scientologists, humanists, etc.

Harassment on the basis of an individual's religion or creed is a violation of Title VII. Mocking one's religious beliefs and customs, making offensive jokes and other negative verbal conduct or actions directed at an individual's beliefs constitutes harassment if it creates an intimidating, hostile or offensive working environment, unreasonably interferes with work performance or negatively affects an individual's employment opportunities.

SEXUAL HARASSMENT

The protected class of "sex" or "gender" refers to the condition or character of being male or female. All people are "male or female" and therefore covered under this category. Sexual orientation is not protected under this or any other protected class identified by Title VII of the 1964 Civil Rights Act, however, it may be protected under other federal, state or local workplace harassment laws.

Sexual harassment in the workplace encompasses a more broad range of behaviors and situations, and is discussed more fully in Chapter 4 of this almanac.

HARASSMENT ON THE BASIS OF NATIONAL ORIGIN

The protected class of "national origin" refers to the particular characteristics of the people of a nation; or relating to the ancestral beginnings, physical, cultural, or linguistic characteristics of a particular national group, such as Italian-Americans, Irish Americans, Colombians, etc.

Harassment on the basis of national origin is also a violation of Title VII. An ethnic slur or other verbal or physical conduct because of an individual's nationality constitutes harassment if it creates an intimidating, hostile or offensive working environment, unreasonably interferes with work performance or negatively affects an individual's employment opportunities.

Harassment may also occur when an employer commits "document abuse." Document abuse occurs when certain employees or applicants are subject to more stringent verification measures than necessary to verify that they are eligible to work in the United States. This can occur when an employer rejects a worker's valid documents, or requests additional documentation beyond what is legally required.

HARASSMENT ON THE BASIS OF DISABILITY

The protected class of "disability" refers to any person who has a physical or mental impairment which substantially limits one or more major life activities; one who has a record of such impairment; or one who is regarded as having such an impairment, such as persons with vision or hearing impairments, epilepsy, paralysis, mental impairment, etc.

Title I of the Americans with Disabilities Act of 1990 prohibits private employers, state and local governments, employment agencies and labor unions from discriminating against qualified individuals with disabilities in job application procedures, hiring, firing, advancement, compensation, job training, and other terms, conditions and privileges of employment.

As with discrimination on the basis of race, color, national origin and religion, the prohibition against workplace harassment is violated where an employee is subjected to verbal insults, jokes and other verbal or physical conduct related to their disability, which creates a hostile or offensive work environment, and unreasonably interferes with work performance or negatively affects an individual's employment opportunities.

HARASSMENT ON THE BASIS OF AGE

The protected class of "age" under the ADEA refers to individuals who are 40 years or older. As with all of the other bases for harassment, workplace harassment occurs if an employee is subjected to verbal insults, jokes and other verbal or physical conduct related to their age, which creates a hostile work environment, and unreasonably interferes with work performance or negatively affects an individual's employment opportunities.

ENFORCEMENT AND REMEDIES

There is a range of remedies available to the aggrieved party who files a discrimination charge, including:

1. Requiring the employer to post a notice to all employees advising them of their rights under the laws the EEOC enforces, and their right to be free from retaliation;

2. Taking corrective or preventive actions to cure or correct the source of the identified discrimination;

3. Requiring nondiscriminatory placement in the position the victim would have occupied if the discrimination had not occurred;

4. Payment of compensatory damages;

5. Payment of back pay, with interest where applicable;

6. Replacement of lost benefits;

7. Placing a stop to the specific discriminatory practices involved; and

8. Recovery of reasonable attorney's fees, expert witness fees, and court costs.

Damages may also be available to compensate for future monetary losses, and for mental anguish and inconvenience. In addition, punitive damages may also be available where intentional discrimination is found, or if an employer acted with malice or reckless indifference. However, punitive damages are not available against the federal, state or local governments.

RETALIATION

Title VII of the Civil Rights Act of 1964, the Age Discrimination in Employment Act, the Americans with Disabilities Act, and the Equal Pay Act prohibit retaliation by an employer, employment agency, or labor organization because an individual has engaged in protected activity. There are three essential elements of a retaliation claim: (1) there was protected activity, e.g., the employee opposed workplace harassment discrimination or participated in a statutory complaint process investigating workplace harassment; (2) the employee was subjected to adverse action; and (3) there was a causal connection between the protected activity and the adverse action.

Protected Activity

If the party charging retaliation explicitly or implicitly communicated that the accused's activity constituted unlawful discrimination, and that the charging party was "opposed" to the discrimination, this would constitute protected activity. For example, if the party charging retaliation had complained to co-workers about the supervisor's harassment of a disabled co-worker, this complaint constitutes "opposition."

The charging party would also be protected against retaliation even if he or she was mistaken about the unlawfulness of the conduct.

If the party charging retaliation participated in the statutory complaint process for their own charge of discrimination, or that of another employee, such participation would also be protected activity. This would include filing a charge, testifying, and assisting or otherwise participating in an investigation, proceeding, hearing, or lawsuit brought under the statutes enforced by the EEOC. The charging party would also be protected against retaliation regardless of the validity or reasonableness of the original allegation of discrimination.

Adverse Action

Significant retaliatory treatment—e.g., a demotion, dismissal, or pay decrease—which is undertaken after the charging party engaged in the protected activity is unlawful where such treatment is reasonably likely to deter such protected activity. Further, there is no requirement that the adverse action materially affect the terms, conditions, or privileges of employment.

For example, following the filing of a charge alleging racial harassment against the charging party's coworkers and supervisor, the charging party's manager asks several employees to keep the charging party under surveillance and report back to the manager on the charging party's activities. This surveillance would be considered an "adverse action" designed to deter protected activity, and is unlawful if it was conducted because of the charging party's protected activity—i.e., filing a charge of racial harassment.

Causal Connection

A causal connection could be established if there is direct evidence that retaliation was a motive for the adverse action. For example, a causal connection could be established if the offender admitted that it undertook the adverse action because of the protected activity, or if the offender expressed bias against the charging party based on the protected activity, and there is evidence linking the statement of bias to the adverse action.

In one such case, the defendant fired the plaintiff after he reluctantly testified in his co-worker's Title VII case about workplace sexual activities in which he participated. The president of the defendant company told the plaintiff at the time of his termination that his testimony was "the most damning" to the defendant's case. The court found that this comment constituted direct evidence of retaliation.

A causal connection may also be established based on circumstantial evidence. For example, if the adverse action took place shortly after the protected activity took place, this could raise an inference that the retaliation was causally connected to the protected activity.

If the accused produces evidence of a legitimate nondiscriminatory reason for taking adverse action against the employee, it must be determined whether the explanation is merely a pretext designed to conceal the retaliation.

Adverse action may also be taken after the employment relationship has ended. Examples of post-employment retaliation include actions that are designed to interfere with the individual's prospects for employment, such as giving an unjustified negative job reference; refusing to provide a job reference; and informing an individual's prospective employer about the individual's protected activity. However, a negative job reference about an individual who engaged in protected activity does not constitute unlawful retaliation unless the reference was based on a retaliatory motive. The truthfulness of the information in the reference may serve as a defense unless there is proof of pretext. In addition, retaliatory acts designed to interfere with an individual's prospects for employment are unlawful regardless of whether they actually cause a prospective employer to refrain from hiring the individual. If retaliation is found, compensatory and punitive damages are available remedies under all of the statutes enforced by the EEOC.

HARASSMENT BASED ON SEXUAL ORIENTATION, STATUS AS A PARENT, MARITAL STATUS AND POLITICAL AFFILIATION

The EEOC does not enforce the protections that prohibit discrimination and harassment based on sexual orientation, status as a parent, marital status and political affiliation. However, laws governing federal employment, such as the Civil Service Reform Act (CSRA), include such prohibitions. Many state and local laws also offer protection to additional classes of employees other than those listed under Title VII, the ADA and the ADEA. Thus, the reader is advised to check the law of his or her own jurisdiction in this regard.

For example, under the CSRA, federal agencies are prohibited from treating employees differently or less favorably on account of their sexual orientation. Employees who believe that a prohibited personnel practice has been committed against them that constitutes unlawful harassment based upon sexual orientation may seek assistance from the Office of Special Counsel and the Merit Systems Protection Board. Employees may not seek relief from the Equal Employment Opportunity Commission or file a discrimination complaint under Title VII because that law does not prohibit discrimination based upon sexual orientation. The CSRA also prohibits retaliation against federal employees or applicants for whistle-blowing, or for exercising an appeal, complaint, or grievance right.

Another federal law which offers greater protection to classes of employees than those covered by Title VII is Executive Order 11478, as amended by Executive Orders 13087 and 13152, which is discussed more fully in Chapter 1 of this almanac.

CHAPTER 4:
SEXUAL HARASSMENT

IN GENERAL

Each year, many women and men experience unlawful sexual harassment at work. The EEOC basically defines sexual harassment as "unwelcome" sexual advances, requests for sexual favors and other verbal or physical conduct of a sexual nature when:

1. Submission to such conduct is made either explicitly or implicitly a term or condition of an individual's employment;

2. Submission to or rejection of such conduct by an individual is used as the basis for employment decisions affecting such individual; or

3. Such conduct has the purpose or effect of unreasonably interfering with an individual's work performance or creating an intimidating, hostile or offensive working environment.

SCOPE OF THE PROBLEM

In 1980, the federal government surveyed its employees and found that forty-two percent of women, and fifteen percent of men, stated they had experienced some form of work-related sexual harassment. When the federal government looked at the same issue seven years later, the numbers had not changed. Surveys done in the private sector revealed similar results. Nevertheless, most cases—as many as 95%—of sexual harassment still go unreported.

The harm caused by sexual harassment to the victim is tremendous. Victims of sexual harassment suffer humiliation, loss of dignity, psychological harm and, in some cases, physical injury. They also suffer damage to their professional reputation and career, and loss of income while they have to make a choice between keeping their job or avoiding the harm. The "trickle down" effect of this scenario is the negative impact on the economy, which cannot be overlooked, particularly given the number of victims. In recent years, the number of sexual harassment cases filed with the EEOC, as well as in federal and state courts, has climbed dramatically.

Studies also show that, in addition to the significant impact sexual harassment has on the individual, the financial cost of sexual harassment to businesses is exorbitant. In the federal government's first sexual harassment survey, it discovered that the government itself had lost $189 million between 1978 and 1980 from the effects of sexual harassment. In its next survey, the federal government saw its losses jump to $267 million for the years 1985 to 1987, even though the rate of sexual harassment had not changed.

According to another study, the losses to the private sector caused by the ramifications of sexual harassment are also quite significant. Losses can result from absenteeism, lower productivity, increased health-care costs, poor morale, and employee turnover. In addition to those costs, there are litigation costs and court-awarded damages. There is also the loss of reputation to a business that is not vigilant in preventing and correcting sexual harassment in the workplace.

GOVERNING LAW

The American court system did not decide the first sexual harassment case under Title VII until 1976, and it was not until 1980 that the EEOC officially stated that sexual harassment was a form of gender discrimination which is prohibited under Title VII. The EEOC then issued regulations defining illegal sexual harassment. In 1986, the U.S. Supreme Court also held that sexual harassment was a form of illegal employment discrimination.

An individual is now generally permitted to bring a claim for sexual harassment under either Title VII, or the applicable state or local law. However, until 1991, Title VII entitled sexual harassment victims to collect only back pay, lost wages and, if they had been forced to leave, to be reinstated in their jobs. Nothing was provided for pain and suffering. In addition to the paltry recovery, these cases were very difficult to win.

Recognizing the need to strengthen the remedies for sexual harassment under Title VII, Congress amended the Civil Rights Act in 1991. Now, sexual harassment victims can recover compensatory damages beyond back pay, and may do so in a jury trial. Moreover, these damages can encompass "future pecuniary losses, emotional pain, suffering, inconvenience, mental anguish, loss of enjoyment of life, and other nonpecuniary losses." Plaintiffs can also collect punitive damages, if they can demonstrate that an employer acted with malice or with reckless or callous indifference. As set forth below, however, the legislation limits the sum of compensatory and punitive damages recoverable.

Limit On Damages

The law limits the sum of compensatory and punitive damages depending on the number of employees. In companies with 15 to 100 employees, the maximum sum of compensatory and punitive damages is $50,000. In companies with 101 to 200 employees, the maximum is $100,000. In companies with 201 to 500 employees, the maximum is $200,000, and in companies with 501 or more employees, the maximum in compensatory and punitive damages recoverable is $300,000.

LEGAL GROUNDS FOR SEXUAL HARASSMENT CLAIMS

As discussed below, federal law recognizes two different sets of legal grounds for claiming sexual harassment under Title VII: (1) Quid Pro Quo; and (2) Hostile Work Environment.

QUID PRO QUO SEXUAL HARASSMENT

Under the quid pro quo form of harassment, a person in authority, usually a supervisor, demands sexual favors of a subordinate as a condition of getting or keeping a job benefit. In quid pro quo cases, the offense is directly linked to an individual's terms of employment or forms the basis for employment decisions affecting the individual. Usually, such cases are easy to recognize. The first sexual harassment lawsuit under Title VII was decided on quid pro quo grounds.

In quid pro quo cases, the conduct of an authority figure will be scrutinized more closely because of the power he or she may have over the employee, such as promotions, etc. It is the perceived threat of requiring sexual favors as the basis for making employment-related decisions that determines whether the conduct constitutes sexual harassment.

When such harassment occurs, the subordinate has the legal right to take the employer to court under the doctrine of "respondeat superior," which makes a company responsible for a supervisor's actions. There is a presumption that the employer has knowledge, or should have knowledge, of the illegal behavior.

In 1988, the EEOC amended its guidelines to extend legal responsibility on employers for the sexual harassment of employees by nonemployees—i.e., agents acting on behalf of the employer—when the employer, its agents or supervisory employees, knew or should have known of the conduct and failed to take appropriate corrective action.

If the sexual advances are made by a co-worker, the determination is less clear because the co-worker generally does not have any "power" over another employee, and cannot threaten the employee with adverse employment actions. Instead, the court will look more at the nature of the behavior, e.g., the language and/or gestures used, the frequency and persistency of the advances, etc., under the hostile work environment standard discussed below

In addition, the presumption of employer knowledge is not applicable when the offender is a co-worker. The employee generally must put the co-worker and the employee "on notice" that the conduct is unwelcome and will not be tolerated. If the employer thereafter does nothing to stop the conduct, then the employer may be liable for the harasser's actions.

THE SEXUALLY OFFENSIVE HOSTILE WORK ENVIRONMENT

Frequently, a quid pro quo situation does not exist. Many sexual harassment victims are never threatened with termination or lack of advancement. Rather, they suffer repeated abuse by a hostile work environment, which is an alternative ground for bringing a Title VII sexual harassment action. A hostile work environment arises when a co-worker or supervisor, engaging in unwelcome and inappropriate sexually based behavior, renders the workplace atmosphere intimidating, hostile, or offensive.

Courts have recognized that creating a sexually offensive work environment—e.g., by displaying pornographic materials in the workplace, or by engaging in vulgar and lewd behavior—is a violation of sexual harassment laws. This is so even if the offensive conduct is not directed at any particular individual. The concern is that the creation of such a sexually offensive atmosphere demeans, and works to the disadvantage of the employees, and in particular, female employees. For example, it is difficult for a female employee to be taken seriously when surrounded by lewd and humiliating representations of naked women.

Thus, in 1986, the U.S. Supreme Court held that sexual harassment, even if it is not linked directly to the grant or denial of an economic quid pro quo, is illegal where "such conduct has the purpose or effect of unreasonably interfering with an individual's work performance or creating an intimidating, hostile, or offensive working environment."

Another issue concerning hostile environment cases is whether a victim may only recover for sexual harassment aimed at the victim, or whether she may cite examples of sex-based conduct directed at other employees to establish her prima facie case. A number of courts have held that incidents involving employees other than the victim are relevant in establishing a generally hostile work environment.

Standards of Conduct

The Supreme Court further held that a hostile work environment constitutes grounds for an action only when the conduct is unwelcome, based on sex, and severe or pervasive enough "to alter the conditions of employment and create an abusive working environment."

Thus, there are three major standards that are examined to determine whether conduct creates a sexually offensive hostile work environment:

The Reasonable Employee Standard

The standard a court usually uses in determining whether conduct violates the law is whether or not a "reasonable" employee would find the conduct offensive. In addition, the individual can set the boundaries of "reasonableness" for themselves by communicating to the offender that he or she finds the behavior offensive. If the offender thereafter persists, he or she will have violated the standard of conduct she set.

The Severe and Pervasive Standard

Another factor a court uses to determine whether certain conduct constitutes sexual harassment is whether the behavior was so severe or pervasive that it created a hostile work environment. According to the EEOC, some factors which indicate that behavior was "severe and pervasive" include: (i) the type of behavior, e.g. whether it was verbal, physical or both; (ii) the frequency of the behavior; (iii) the position of the offender, e.g., supervisor or co-worker; (iv) the number of individuals who engaged in such behaviors; and (v) whether the behavior was directed at one or more individuals.

Of course, certain types of behavior do not have to be cumulative, but need only occur once to be deemed illegal, e.g. employment or promotions that are conditioned on sexual favors, or outright sexual attacks.

When investigating allegations of sexual harassment, the EEOC looks at the whole record: the circumstances, such as the nature of the sexual advances, and the context in which the alleged incidents occurred. A determination on the allegations is made from the facts on a case-by-case basis.

The Unwelcome Conduct Standard

Although it may appear that any behavior which gives rise to a complaint would qualify as "unwelcome," the court may examine additional criteria to make its determination, such as whether the behavior was unwelcome at the time it occurred.

For example, an individual may have engaged in sexual behavior with a co-worker voluntarily at one time. However, if thereafter the individual has communicated their desire not to continue in such a relationship, any subsequent sexual demands placed upon the individual would be deemed "unwelcome" and would likely constitute illegal sexual harassment.

In addition, even if the individual "voluntarily" goes along with the offensive behavior, if he or she does so out of fear of losing their job, this would also constitute "unwelcome" behavior.

Employer Liability in Sexually Hostile Work Environment Cases

In sexual harassment cases based on a hostile work environment, employers are not always automatically liable for their supervisors' conduct. Under the EEOC guidelines, employers are liable when either their supervisors or agents create a hostile environment, or if the employer knew or should have known of the sexual harassment and failed to take immediate and appropriate corrective action.

According to the EEOC, employers are usually deemed to know of sexual harassment if it is: (1) openly practiced in the workplace; (2) well-known among employees; or (3) brought to the employer's notice when a victim files a charge.

As further discussed in Chapter 6, employers may protect themselves from liability by taking immediate and appropriate corrective action. To do so, companies need to institute comprehensive, detailed, and explicit sexual harassment policies. The Supreme Court held that where an employer's general nondiscrimination policy did not address sexual harassment in particular, it did not alert employees to their employer's interest in correcting that form of discrimination.

Moreover, the Court found that where an employer's grievance procedure required an employee to complain first to their supervisor, who in that case happened to be the perpetrator of the harassment, the employee's failure to invoke the employer's internal procedures was not unreasonable and the employer could not use this as a defense.

Examples of Sexually Hostile Work Environments

The following cases illustrate conduct that creates a hostile work environment:

In one case, a construction company hired three women to work as traffic controllers at road construction sites. Male co-workers immediately and continually subjected the women to outrageous verbal sexual abuse. One of the three women developed a skin reaction to the sun and the men nicknamed her "Herpes." When the women returned to their car after work one day, they found obscenities written in the dust on their car. Male co-workers continuously asked the woman if they wanted to engage in sexual intercourse or oral sex. The men subjected all three woman to other types of abuse, including "mooning" them, showing them pornographic pictures, and urinating in their water bottles and automobile gas tanks. The company's supervisor was well aware of all of these activities. The court found this conduct violated Title VII because it was unwelcome conduct of a sexual nature, even though it did not contain "explicit sexual overtones."

In another case, a shipyard company employed a female welder who was continually subjected to nude and partially nude pictures posted by her male co-workers. The men posted these pictures not only in common areas, but also in places where the victim would have to encounter them, including her tool box. The men referred to the victim as "baby," "sugar," "momma," and "dear." In addition, the men wrote obscene graffiti directed at the victim all over the plant. The men also made numerous suggestive and offensive remarks to the victim concerning her body and the pictures posted on the walls. The victim complained about this atmosphere of harassment on a number of occasions, but the company's supervisory personnel provided little or no assistance. The court found this conduct violated Title VII because the plaintiff belonged to a protected category, was subject to unwelcome sexual harassment, the harassment was based on sex, it affected a term or condition of her employment, and the employer knew or should have known about the harassment and failed to take remedial action.

In another case, harassment of the victim began when a co-worker broadcast over the company's public address system obscenities about the female victim, who then received over thirty pornographic notes in her locker. The men covered the walls of the facility and the elevator with pornographic pictures and crude remarks concerning the victim. In addition, one of the victim's supervisors told her that she should have sex with a certain co-worker, and he also physically accosted her. Another employee told the victim that "he would cut off her left breast and shove it down her throat." On another occasion, this same employee held the victim "over a stairwell, more than thirty feet from the floor." Other male employees also physically grabbed and pinched the victim. The court found this conduct stated a claim of hostile environment discrimination under Title VII, because employees touched her in a sexual manner, directed sexual comments toward her, and continued to write sexual graffiti throughout the workplace.

MALE SEXUAL HARASSMENT

Most people assume that sexual harassment complaints are always brought by women who suffer at the hands of their male co-workers and supervisors. This is not true. Sexual harassment on the job is unwanted, abusive behavior regardless of gender. Women, as well as men, engage in unlawful sexual harassment in order to intimidate or humiliate their male counterparts. It is also entirely possible for women to harass women and men to harass men on the job.

The most recent statistics available show a steady increase in the percentage of claims that men have filed with the EEOC—up from 7.5% in 1991 to about 12% in 1999. The Courts have recognized that sexual harassment is a gender neutral offense. In addition, it is expected that there will be an ever greater increase in male complaints since the U.S. Supreme Court's recent recognition of same sex harassment, as further discussed below.

SAME-SEX HARASSMENT

Courts are split on the issue of same-sex harassment in the workplace. Some courts have held that same-sex sexual harassment claims are not recognized under such non-discrimination statutes as Title VII. Some have concluded that same-sex claims should only proceed where the affected employee can prove that the harasser is homosexual and therefore motivated by a personal sexual interest. Other courts have suggested that workplace harassment that is sexual in content is always actionable, regardless of the harasser's sex, sexual orientation or motivation.

In 1998, in a unanimous opinion that impacts workplaces across the country, the U.S. Supreme Court resolved any doubt on the issue:

> Nothing in Title VII necessarily bars a claim of discrimination "because of . . . sex" merely because the complaining employee and the alleged harasser are both of the same sex. *Oncale v. Sundowner Offshore*

Services, Inc., 523 U.S.75; 118 S.Ct. 998; 140 L. Ed. 2d 201; 66 U.S.L.W. 4172.

In *Oncale*, the plaintiff worked with an eight man crew on a Chevron USA oil platform in the Gulf of Mexico. Three of the other crew members, including two supervisors, forcibly subjected Oncale, on numerous occasions, to sex-related humiliating actions in the presence of the rest of the crew. The two supervisors physically assaulted him in a sexual manner and one of the supervisors threatened Oncale with rape.

Oncale complained to his supervisor, to no avail. Oncale ultimately quit as a result of the harassment and verbal abuse. He testified in his deposition that he thought if he didn't leave his job he would be raped or forced to have sex.

Oncale's subsequent lawsuit in Louisiana federal court was summarily dismissed based on the existing law in the 5th Circuit that a male has no cause of action under Title VII for harassment by male coworkers. The 5th Circuit affirmed the trial court's dismissal and Oncale took his case to the U.S. Supreme Court.

The Supreme Court held that Title VII's prohibition of discrimination because of sex protects men as well as women. As guidance, the Court looked to the law of racial discrimination in which it is clear that an employer can discriminate against members of its own race, and the law which provides that a male employee can claim that an employer discriminated against him because of his sex when it selected a female employee for promotion.

Thus, men and women are now equally protected by the sex discrimination provisions of the federal statute. Courts faced with same-sex cases will be expected, under the Supreme Court's standard, to examine all the facts and circumstances. As in opposite sex cases, conduct that is not severe or pervasive enough to create an objectively hostile or abusive work environment does not violate Title VII.

CONFRONTING SEXUAL HARASSMENT

The first step to take in confronting sexual harassment in the workplace is to tell the harasser that his or her behavior is illegal and it must stop immediately. This is particularly effective when the harassment is at a fairly low level. It would also be prudent to document the harassment, as further set forth in Chapter 8 of this almanac.

If the harasser continues the behavior after having been told to stop, the employee may have to resort to the Company's internal complaint procedure to end the harassment. It is important to determine whether there is an established sexual harassment policy and follow the procedures outlined. As more fully set forth in Chapter 6, an employee's unreasonable failure to follow an employer's internal complaint procedure, which would put the employer on notice, and give the employer the chance to correct the conduct, may be fatal to any subsequent lawsuit against the employer.

If the employer has not established a formal internal complaint procedure, the employee should still put the employer on notice of the harassment, either in writing or by requesting a formal meeting with the appropriate human resources officer.

In preparation for making a complaint, one should gather as much evidence as possible about the harassment, including offensive letters, photographs, cards or notes that may have been sent. If possible, any pornography, lewd cartoons, or other offensive materials that may have been displayed or distributed in the public workplace should be confiscated. Also, as set forth more fully in Chapter 8, the employee should keep a detailed journal, and retain copies of every document contained in their personnel file.

If all internal efforts to resolve the harassment fail, the next step would be to consider litigation. Some jurisdictions may require the victim to first file with the EEOC or the governing state agency prior to taking legal action. If the EEOC is unable to resolve the claim, they may issue the employee a right-to-sue letter enabling them to file a lawsuit in court. Information on filing a charge and obtaining the right to sue for workplace harassment is discussed in Chapter 7 of this almanac.

Because state and local laws may provide greater protection to the employee, the reader is advised to check the law in his or her own jurisdiction in this regard.

THE U.S. DEPARTMENT OF LABOR—WOMEN'S BUREAU

The Women's Bureau, part of the U.S. Department of Labor, was created by Congress in 1920. Their mission is to research and promote policies to improve working conditions for women. The Women's Bureau provides information to women about their rights in the workplace. In addition to the information provided by the EEOC, the reader is advised to contact their regional office for more information on sex discrimination in the workplace, including sexual harassment.

A directory of Women's Bureau Regional Offices of the U.S. Department of Labor is set forth at Appendix 7.

CHAPTER 5:
WORKPLACE HARASSMENT
POST-SEPTEMBER 11TH

IN GENERAL

Since the attacks of September 11, 2001, the Equal Employment Opportunity Commission (EEOC) and state and local fair employment practices agencies (FEPAs) have reported a significant increase in the number of charges alleging discrimination based on national origin and/or religion. Not surprisingly, many of the charges have been filed by individuals who are, or are perceived to be, from Muslim, Arab, Middle Eastern, South Asian, or Sikh backgrounds. These charges most commonly allege harassment and discharge.

Although employers are already under an obligation to prevent and correct employment discrimination, as discussed in this almanac, due to the events of September 11th, employers and labor unions may have to increase their efforts in preventing harassment in the workplace of certain target groups. Anger at those responsible for the tragic events of September 11th should not be misdirected against innocent individuals because of their religion or ethnicity.

Further, as set forth below, many types of discrimination and harassment are implicated by this situation. Many races, national origins, ethnic backgrounds, religious beliefs, and other potentially protected categories are possible targets of discrimination. The EEOC guidelines, reiterated in a press release urging tolerance in the wake of the September 11th attacks, identify the following bases for unlawful workplace bias relevant to the current situation:

1. Religion, ethnicity, birthplace, culture, or linguistic characteristics;

2. Marriage or association with persons of a national origin or religious group;

---

3. Membership or association with specific ethnic or religious groups;

4. Physical, linguistic, or cultural traits closely associated with a national origin group; for example, discrimination because of a person's physical features or traditional Arab style of dress; and

5. Perception or belief that a person is a member of a particular national origin group, based on the person's speech, mannerisms, or appearance.

THE HOSTILE WORK ENVIRONMENT

An unfortunate occurrence following the aftermath of September 11th is that many Arab-Americans who had positive and even friendly relationships with co-workers have encountered suspicion, tension and hostility in the workplace. Many have been unfairly subjected to racial epithets and insults. These individuals often feel helpless because they cannot undo the horror of September 11th, and they are as innocent as their fellow co-workers in what happened that day. It is merely because of their ethnicity and/or religion that suspicion has been cast upon them, and they, like most employees, cannot simply leave their employment.

It is important that an employee faced with such a situation try to speak openly with their employer about their dilemma, and try to come up with solutions to the problem. It may be prudent to hold a meeting among the co-workers to discuss the situation, where everyone can air their opinions and openly discuss their feelings. This may be particularly helpful if the employee previously had a good working relationship with his or her co-workers. Open communication may reduce or eliminate the tension and suspicions that may be fueling the situation.

Nevertheless, if all options fail, employees who are being targeted because of their ethnicity and/or religion should pursue all legal remedies, particularly if the employer is made aware of the situation and does not intervene to take any corrective measures to stop the illegal harassment.

RELIGIOUS APPAREL

An employer cannot require an employee to remove religious apparel that is necessary for the employee to wear to conform with their religious beliefs, such as the traditional turban worn by Sikh men, or the "hijab,"—a traditional head scarf worn by Muslim women. This would violate Title VII even if the employer fears that the employee's religious attire would create an atmosphere of hostility among co-workers, or would discourage clients or customers from doing business with the employer.

An employer cannot refuse to hire a person because customers or co-workers may be "uncomfortable" with that person's religion or national origin. In addition, the employer cannot reassign the employee to another work location in order to "hide" the employee. For example, if the employee is a front desk receptionist, the employer cannot force the employee to take another assignment out of public view. Similarly, an employer may not fire someone, or take any type of punitive employment actions involving the employee, simply because of their religion and/or national origin.

Such concerns, whether real or perceived, do not establish undue hardship and can never justify discrimination. Thus, even if the employer has established a dress code, an exception must be made to permit the employee to wear religiously-mandated attire as a religious accommodation. If coworkers, who may be sensitive to Arab-American customs following September 11th, create a hostile work environment for the employee by ridiculing and/or otherwise making the employee uncomfortable because of their religious apparel, those employees must be dealt with according to the law prohibiting workplace harassment.

ASSOCIATION AND AFFILIATION

It is also unlawful to harass an individual because of their association or relationship with a person or organization who is a member of one of the target groups. For example, it is illegal to harass an individual because their spouse is Arab, or because they attend a mosque.

THE DEPARTMENT OF JUSTICE INITIATIVE TO COMBAT THE POST-9/11 DISCRIMINATORY BACKLASH

The Assistant Attorney General for Civil Rights has directed the Civil Rights Division of the Department of Justice to help combat violations of federal civil rights laws affecting individuals perceived to be Arab American, Muslim American, Sikh American, or South-Asian American.

The Civil Rights Division will seek to combat discrimination by: (1) receiving reports of violations based on national origin, citizenship status and religion, including those related to employment; (2) referring them to the appropriate federal authorities; (3) conducting outreach to vulnerable communities to provide them with information about Department of Justice services and connect them with other government agencies that can assist them; and (4) working with other Department of Justice components and other governmental agencies to ensure accurate referral, effective outreach and provision of services to victims of civil rights violations.

For more information on discrimination against Muslims, Arabs, South Asians and Sikhs in the aftermath of September 11, 2001, the reader may refer to the Department of Justice Initiative to Combat Post-9/11 Backlash by visiting the agency's internet website located at http://www.usdoj.gov/>.

THE OFFICE OF SPECIAL COUNSEL FOR IMMIGRATION RELATED UNFAIR EMPLOYMENT PRACTICES

Since the September 11 terrorist attacks against the United States, the Civil Rights Division of the U.S. Department of Justice has received a substantial number of reports of discrimination, as well as threats and violence against persons of Arab, Middle Eastern or South Asian descent, including Sikhs and Muslims. In the workplace, individuals have encountered discriminatory hiring practices, hostile working environments, and terminations because they are a member of one of these target groups.

The Office of Special Counsel for Immigration Related Unfair Employment Practices (OSC) has been addressing many of these workplace discrimination violations, and advises employers, supervisors and employees to be especially vigilant to guard against unfair treatment of persons perceived to be of Middle Eastern descent.

The OSC also handles employment discrimination claims related to an individual's immigration or citizenship status, and investigates charges of document abuse. Document abuse is a type of harassment where the employer requests an employee or job applicant to establish employment eligibility and identity by presenting more or different documents than are required by law, or where the employer rejects reasonably genuine-looking documents, etc.

A witness or subject in an OSC investigation may choose to have personal legal counsel present at the OSC investigative interview. The individual must arrange for their own legal representation. The OSC will not recommend, designate or arrange for representation for any witness or subject. Individuals who choose to have legal counsel accompany them to the OSC interview must complete a designation of representation form, and the legal representative must indicate their agreement to such designation by signing the form.

A copy of the OSC Designation of Representation Form is set forth at Appendix 8.

The OSC has staff available to answer questions employment discrimination and workplace harassment involving target groups post-9/11. The OSC has access to translation services in 116 languages, including Arabic, Urdu, Hindi, Farsi and other languages spoken by individuals from the Middle East and South Asia.

OSC contact information for employers and employees is as follows:

Office of Special Counsel for Immigration Related Unfair Employment Practices
P.O. Box 27728
Washington, D.C. 20038-7728
Toll-Free Automated Employer Hotline: 1-800-255-8155
Toll-Free Number: 1-800-255-7688
TDD for the Hearing Impaired: 1-800-237-2515

Website: http://www.usdoj.gov/crt/osc

CHAPTER 6:
EMPLOYER LIABILITY FOR WORKPLACE HARASSMENT AND THE EMPLOYEE'S DUTY TO EXERCISE REASONABLE CARE

IN GENERAL

Private employers, as well as state and local governments and public or private educational institutions, employment agencies, labor unions, and apprentice programs are subject to the equal opportunity laws prohibiting workplace harassment.

An employer is generally liable for workplace harassment by their employees, including supervisors and co-workers, if the employer knew, or should have known, of the harassment and did nothing to prevent or stop the abusive practices and behavior.

An employer is always responsible for harassment by a supervisor that culminates in a "tangible employment action." This was the holding by the United States Supreme Court in *Burlington Industries, Inc. v. Ellerth*, 118 S. Ct. 2257 (1998), and *Faragher v. City of Boca Raton*, 118 S. Ct. 2275 (1998).

The Court based the standard of liability on two principles:

1. An employer is responsible for the acts of its supervisors; and

2. Employers should be encouraged to prevent harassment, and employees should be encouraged to avoid or limit the harm from harassment.

Thus, although the Court held that an employer is always liable for a supervisor's harassment if it culminates in a tangible employment action, it also held that the employer may be able to avoid liability or limit damages by establishing an affirmative defense based on the following two necessary elements:

1. The employer exercised reasonable care to prevent and correct promptly any harassing behavior, and

---

2. The employee unreasonably failed to take advantage of any preventive or corrective opportunities provided by the employer or to avoid harm otherwise.

This affirmative defense demonstrates the policy of the antiharassment statutes to deter harassment, and rewards employers who take such preventive measures, and is discussed in more detail below.

TANGIBLE EMPLOYMENT ACTION

A "tangible employment action" means a significant change in employment status. Examples of a tangible employment action include: (i) hiring; (ii) firing; (iii) promotion; (iv) demotion; (v) undesirable reassignment; (vi) a decision causing a significant change in benefits; (vii) compensation decisions, and (viii) work assignment.

Harassment which culminates in a tangible employment action may occur, for example, if a supervisor fires or demotes a subordinate because he or she rejects the supervisor's sexual demands, or promotes the employee because he or she submits to the supervisor's sexual demands.

In the *Ellerth* and *Faragher* cases, the Supreme Court held that when a supervisor sexually harasses an employee and the harassment results in a "tangible employment decision" "such as discharge, demotion or undesirable reassignment, the employer has violated federal law. Other types of illegal sexual harassment by supervisors and managers are treated as hostile environment harassment.

In cases of hostile environment harassment, the employer will not be held responsible for harassment by its supervisors if it: (1) exercised reasonable care to prevent and correct promptly any sexually harassing behavior; and (2) the victims of harassment unreasonably failed to take advantage of any preventive or corrective opportunities provided by the employer.

TYPES OF UNLAWFUL HARASSMENT

Although the *Faragher* and *Ellerth* decisions involved sexual harassment complaints, the Court's decision relied on standards set forth in cases involving other types of harassment. This is in line with the EEOC's position that the same standards apply to unlawful harassment based on race, color, sex, religion, national origin, disability, or protected activity under the anti-discrimination statutes. Thus, employers should establish anti-harassment policies and complaint procedures covering all forms of unlawful harassment.

SUPERVISORY CAPACITY

As set forth above, the employer is vicariously liable for unlawful harassment committed by its supervisors against the employees they manage. In general, an individual is considered an employee's "supervisor" if:

1. The individual has the authority to recommend tangible employment decisions affecting the employee; or

2. If the individual has the authority to direct the employee's daily work activities.

Even if the individual's authority to recommend tangible employment decisions is subject to review by higher level supervisors, the individual would still be deemed a supervisor if their recommendations carried sufficient weight in such decisions.

In addition, even if that individual does not have the authority to undertake or recommend tangible job decisions, an individual who is authorized to direct another employee's day-to-day work activities qualifies as his or her supervisor because their ability to commit harassment is enhanced by their authority to increase the employee's workload or assign undesirable tasks.

Another factor in determining whether one is in a supervisory "chain of command" above the employee is whether they have immediate, or successively higher, authority over the employee. However, even if the individual was not in the employee's supervisory chain of command, if the employee perceived that the individual had broad powers where they could have some affect on the employee's conditions of employment, the employer may still be vicariously liable for that individual's actions.

Further, an individual who is temporarily authorized to direct another employee's daily work activities qualifies as his or her "supervisor" during that time period. However, if the offender had no actual supervisory power over the employee, and the employee did not reasonably believe that he or she had such authority, then the standard of liability for co-worker harassment applies.

BACKGROUND INVESTIGATION

An employer should carefully screen applicants for supervisory positions to determine whether they have had any history of harassment complaints against them. If an employer hires such an individual, and they could have readily discovered the supervisor's background, they may be subject to liability for negligence in hiring that person.

If the employer hires the applicant in a supervisory position despite their background, they should fully inform the individual of the employer's anti-harassment policy, and take all appropriate steps to monitor the supervisor's actions and prevent any future harassment. An employer should keep records of harassment complaints and check those records when a complaint of harassment is made to reveal any patterns of harassment by the same individuals.

REASONABLE CARE TO PREVENT AND CORRECT HARASSMENT

The required reasonable care an employer needs to demonstrate in order to avoid or limit liability for workplace harassment generally requires the employer to take reasonable steps to prevent and correct harassment.

Preventive Measures

Anti-Harassment Policy

Employers should establish and enforce a policy prohibiting harassment and setting out a procedure for making complaints. Preferably, the policy and procedure should be in writing and posted in a conspicuous area in the place of employment. The policy and complaint procedure should be written in a way that will be understood by all employees in the employer's workforce. An employer should also provide every employee with a copy of the policy and complaint procedure, and redistribute it periodically. If feasible, the employer should incorporate the policy and complaint procedure into employee handbooks, and provide training to all employees to ensure that they understand their rights and responsibilities.

An effective anti-harassment policy and complaint procedure should contain, at a minimum, the following elements:

1. A clear statement that the employer will not tolerate harassment based on race, sex, religion, national origin, age, or disability, or harassment based on opposition to discrimination, or participation in complaint proceedings.

2. Assurance that employees who make complaints of harassment or provide information related to such complaints will be protected against retaliation, and that the employer will not tolerate retaliation against anyone who complains of harassment or who participates in an investigation;

3. A clearly described complaint process that provides accessible avenues of complaint;

4. Assurance that the employer will protect the confidentiality of harassment complaints to the extent possible;

5. A complaint process that provides a prompt, thorough, and impartial investigation; and

6. Assurance that the employer will take immediate and appropriate corrective action when it determines that harassment has occurred.

A sample workplace harassment policy is set forth at Appendix 9.

Establishing Internal Complaint Procedures

An employer should encourage its employees to report harassment to management before it becomes severe or pervasive. The employer should designate the persons who will take such complaints, and ensure that these individuals are accessible to the employees. The employer should also instruct all of its supervisors to report complaints of harassment to appropriate officials, and assure employees that it will protect their confidentiality to the extent possible.

It is not appropriate to require employees to first report harassment complaints to their immediate supervisors insofar as the immediate supervisor may not be impartial. Also, in many scenarios, it is the immediate supervisor who is accused of the harassment.

Once a complaint is made, the employer must conduct a prompt, thorough, and impartial investigation of the complaint and undertake swift and appropriate corrective action in order to fulfill its responsibility to "effectively prevent and correct harassment." Due care also requires the employer to address complaints made outside of the official complaint procedure.

For example, if an employee files a charge with the EEOC alleging unlawful harassment without notifying the employer, the employer should launch an internal investigation even though the employee did not utilize the employer's internal complaint process.

During the investigation, the accused should not have any direct or indirect control over the investigation. The investigator should interview the employee, the accused, and others who could reasonably be expected to have relevant information.

Pending the outcome, the employer must make sure that the harassment does not continue. This may be a challenging task. For example, it may be unlawful to unfairly burden the complainant by transferring him or her involuntarily, as this may be deemed to be a retaliatory action. Alternatives may include scheduling changes, or placing the accused on some type of non-disciplinary leave with pay pending resolution of the claim.

Monitoring The Workplace

Employers should also be aware of potential problems before a complaint needs to be filed. For example, if there are racial slurs written in the bathroom stalls, or sexually offensive posters hanging on the cafeteria bulletin board, the employer should take immediate steps to have the offensive material removed or erased.

Corrective Measures

If the investigation concludes that there has been unlawful harassment, the employer should take immediate steps to stop the behavior and make sure it does not happen again. Depending on the seriousness of the behavior, disciplinary measures should be undertaken. The employer should also correct any negative effects the harassment may have caused the employee, such as restoring any salary decreases and expunging negative performance evaluations, etc.

THE CHARGING EMPLOYEE'S DUTY TO EXERCISE REASONABLE CARE

The law also places some responsibility on the employee to exercise reasonable care to avoid harassment and try to minimize their damages. If an employee fails to do so, the employer may be able to avoid or limit their liability for workplace harassment. However, the employer must show that the employee "unreasonably failed to take advantage of any preventive or corrective opportunities provided by the employer or to avoid harm otherwise."

Thus an employer who exercised the necessary degree of reasonable care to prevent harassment, as set forth above, is not liable for unlawful harassment if the employee could have avoided all of the actionable harm. If some but not all of the harm could have been avoided, then an award of damages will be mitigated accordingly.

For example, if the employee could not support his or her allegation of harassment, was untruthful, or otherwise failed to cooperate in the investigation, the complaint would not qualify as an effort to avoid harm. Further, if the employee unreasonably delayed making the complaint, where an earlier complaint could have reduced the employee's harm, the employer's liability could be limited.

Failure to Complain

A determination as to whether an employee unreasonably failed to complain or otherwise avoid harm depends on the particular circumstances and information available to the employee at that time. For example, an employee may not report minor episodes of harassment, particularly if it was a first-time occurrence. It would also be reasonable for an employee to try and put up with a certain degree of harassment before they find it necessary to complain. However, if an employee ignores persistent and serious harassment, an unexplainable delay may be deemed unreasonable.

Nevertheless, the circumstances set forth below may excuse the employee's delay in making a complaint.

Risk of Retaliation or Ineffectiveness of Complaint Procedure

If an employee reasonably feared retaliation, an employer would not be able to establish that the employee unreasonably failed to use the complaint procedure. According to the EEOC, employees who are subjected to harassment frequently do not complain to management due to fear of retaliation. Thus, an employer must emphasize its position that retaliation for making a complaint will not be tolerated.

In addition, if the employee's failure or delay in filing a complaint was based on a reasonable belief that the process would be ineffective, the employee's delay may be excused. For example, it would be reasonable for an employee to believe that the complaint process is ineffective if it required the employee to make their initial complaint to their immediate supervisor, who was the offender. A reasonable basis for failure or delay in filing a complaint could also be found if the employee had knowledge of situations where a co-worker's complaints failed to stop harassment.

Other Efforts to Avoid Harm

If the employee made other efforts to avoid harm, the employer would not be able to demonstrate that the employee unreasonably failed to prevent the harassment and minimize their damages. For example, an employee would fulfill their responsibility if they promptly filed a complaint with the EEOC, even though they bypassed the employer's complaint procedure. Filing a grievance with the employee's union could also qualify as a reasonable effort to avoid harm.

PERSONAL LIABILITY OF THE OFFENDER

As demonstrated below, there is a split among jurisdictions as to whether employees, including supervisors and co-workers, can be held individually liable for workplace harassment. Thus, the reader is advised to check the law of his or her own jurisdiction to determine whether individual employees, including supervisors and/or co-workers, are held personally liable for workplace harassment.

In April, 2001, the Washington Supreme Court held that under the state's law against discrimination, supervisors who discriminate against or harass an employee can be held individually liable for their actions. The Washington law prohibits "employers" from discriminating against any person in terms of employment based on age, sex, marital status, race, creed, color, national origin or disability. The law defines "employer" as "any person acting in the interest of an employer, directly or indirectly, who employs eight or more persons . . . "

The court held that this definition intended to include individual supervisors and managers within the term "employer," and was consistent with the broad public policy of eliminating all discrimination in employment. Thus, in Washington, employees can now hold their supervisors personally liable for their actions. This puts an even greater emphasis on employers to implement effective anti-discrimination/anti-harassment training programs and policies for their supervisors.

The California legislature recently took an even more proactive anti-harassment stand by passing an amendment to the California Fair Employment and Housing Act. Under the amendment, all employees, including nonsupervisory co-workers, are subject to individual liability for workplace harassment, including sexual harassment, regardless of whether the employer knew or should have known about the harassment.

The prior law did not hold nonsupervisory employees liable for harassment, and only held the employer liable for workplace harassment by nonsupervisory employees if the employer knew, or should have known, about the conduct and did nothing to prevent, stop or correct the behavior. Under the new law, the jury could find the individual employee liable and award damages, and find the employer not liable.

These laws are in direct contradiction to the federal law set forth by the 9th Circuit, which maintains individuals are not considered "employers" under Title VII of the Civil Rights Act, and thus are immune from personal liability for discrimination and harassment. This holding pertains to both co-workers and supervisors.

THE EEOC SMALL BUSINESS LIAISONS

The EEOC has established small business liaison offices for employers who have questions about the laws enforced by EEOC or about compliance with those laws in specific workplace situations.

A directory of EEOC Small Business Liaisons is set forth at Appendix 10.

Employers may also contact the EEOC's Office of Legal Counsel for informal guidance on workplace harassment matters. Written inquiries should be addressed to:

Office of Legal Counsel
U.S. Equal Employment Opportunity Commission
1801 L Street N.W.
Washington, D.C. 20507

CHAPTER 7:
FILING A CHARGE AND OBTAINING THE RIGHT TO SUE

IN GENERAL

As discussed in this almanac, an individual who believes they have been harassed by an employer, labor union or employment agency, because of their race, color, national origin, sex, age, religion, or disability, may file a discrimination charge with the Equal Employment Opportunity Commission (EEOC). In addition, an individual, organization, or agency may file a charge on behalf of another person in order to protect the aggrieved person's identity. The EEOC is also empowered to initiate a charge if it believes the law has been violated.

Discrimination charges may be filed in person, by mail, or by telephone. The EEOC is headquartered in Washington, D.C., and operates 50 field offices throughout the United States. Individuals seeking to file a charge may contact their nearest EEOC field office, or contact EEOC headquarters at (TEL:) 800-669-4000/(TDD): 800669-6820 for further instructions on filing the charge. If an individual is going to need some type of special assistance in filing the charge, such as an interpreter, they should give the EEOC advance notice of such need.

A Directory of EEOC Offices is set forth at Appendix 1.

In filing a discrimination charge, the charging party will be required to supply the EEOC with the following information:

1. The charging party's name, address and telephone number;

2. The name, address, and telephone number of the respondent employer, employment agency, or union that is alleged to have discriminated, and the number of employees or union members, if known;

3. A short description of the discriminatory act which is alleged to have violated the law;

4. The date of the alleged violation.

TIME LIMITATIONS

There are strict time frames in which charges of employment discrimination must be filed with the EEOC. The charging party must adhere to these filing deadlines in order to protect their right to have the EEOC act on their behalf, and to preserve their right to file a private lawsuit if the EEOC is unable to reach a reasonable settlement of the charge. If a charge is not filed timely, the individual may lose all rights to recover against the offending employer.

Under Title VII and the ADA, discrimination charges must be filed with the EEOC within 180 days of the alleged discriminatory act before the individual is entitled to file a private lawsuit.

In states or localities where there is an anti-discrimination law and an agency authorized to grant or seek relief—known as a Fair Employment Practices Agencies (FEPA)—the charge must be presented to that state or local agency instead of the EEOC. In that case, the individual's time for filing with the EEOC is extended to 300 days from the date of the discriminatory act, or within 30 days after receiving notice that the state or local agency has terminated its processing of the charge, whichever comes first.

When a charge is filed with a state or local FEPA, and is also covered by federal law, the FEPA "dual files" the charge with the EEOC to protect the charging party's federal rights. The charge will usually be retained by the FEPA for handling. If a charge is filed with the EEOC and is also covered by state or local law, the EEOC "dual files" the charge with the state or local FEPA, but ordinarily retains the charge for handling.

THE EEOC MEDIATION PROGRAM

The EEOC investigation process begins after the charge has been filed. The employer is notified that the charge has been filed. A charge may be assigned for priority investigation if the initial facts appear to support a violation of law. When the evidence is less strong, the charge may be assigned for follow up investigation to determine whether it is likely that a violation has occurred.

However, prior to beginning the formal investigation, a case may be selected for the EEOC's mediation program. Mediation is a form of alternative dispute resolution (ADR) that is offered by the EEOC as an alternative to the traditional investigative or litigation process. Mediation is an informal process in which a neutral third party—the mediator—assists the opposing parties in reaching a voluntary, negotiated resolution of a charge of discrimination.

Not all charges are selected for mediation. The EEOC evaluates each charge to determine whether it is appropriate for mediation considering such factors as the nature of the case, the relationship of the parties, the size and complexity of the case, and the relief sought by the charging party. In addition, charges that the EEOC has determined to be without merit are not eligible for mediation.

If mediation is deemed appropriate, it will usually be offered early in the processing of the charge, as an alternative to a lengthy investigation. An EEOC representative will contact the employee and employer concerning their interest in participating in the program. If both parties agree, a mediation session is scheduled. The majority of mediations are completed in one session, which usually lasts from one to five hours. There is no cost to the parties in selecting the mediation process.

While it is not necessary to have an attorney in order to participate in the mediation program, either party may choose to do so. Persons attending the mediation session must have the authority to resolve the dispute. Participation in the mediation program is confidential, voluntary, and requires consent from both the charging party and employer.

Mediation gives the parties the opportunity to discuss the issues raised in the charge, clear up misunderstandings, determine the underlying interests or concerns, find areas of agreement and, ultimately, to incorporate those areas of agreement into resolutions. The mediator does not resolve the charge or impose a decision on the parties. Instead, the mediator helps the parties to agree on a mutually acceptable resolution.

Settlement agreements secured during mediation do not constitute an admission by the employer of any violation of the law. However, an agreement reached during mediation is enforceable in court just like any other settlement agreement resolving a charge of discrimination filed with the EEOC.

The EEOC's mediation program is administered primarily through its field offices, including the Washington Field Office and 24 District Offices, located throughout the country. Each field office has a staff member who is responsible for coordinating mediation activities for discrimination charges filed within that office's geographical jurisdiction.

A directory of EEOC Mediation Offices is set forth at Appendix 5.

THE EEOC INVESTIGATION PROCESS

If a charge is not selected for the mediation process, or mediation is not successful, the charge is returned to an EEOC investigative unit, and continues to be processed and investigated just like any other charge.

In investigating a charge, the EEOC may make written requests for information, interview people, review documents, and, as needed, visit the facility where the alleged discrimination occurred. Because the entire mediation process is strictly confidential, information revealed during the mediation session cannot be disclosed to anyone, including other EEOC personnel. Thus, such information cannot be used during any subsequent investigation.

The investigation may conclude that there is reasonable cause to believe discrimination has taken place, or that there has been no violation of the law, in which case the charge will be dismissed. If the investigation determines that there has been no violation of the law, and that further investigation will not establish a violation of the law, the charge may be dismissed.

If, during their investigation, the EEOC determines there is "reasonable cause" to believe that the alleged discrimination has occurred, it will try to settle the charge between the charging party and the employer. In addition, the EEOC can assist in settling a charge at any stage of the investigation if the charging party and the employer express their interest in doing so. If the EEOC is unable to effectuate a settlement, the investigation continues to completion.

After the investigation has been completed, if the evidence establishes that discrimination has occurred, the employer and the charging party will be informed of this finding in an explanatory letter of determination. The EEOC will then attempt conciliation with the employer to develop a remedy for the discrimination.

If the case is successfully conciliated, neither the EEOC nor the charging party may go to court unless the conciliation agreement is not honored. If the EEOC is unable to successfully conciliate the case, the agency will decide whether to bring suit in federal court. If the EEOC either dismisses the case, or decides not to sue, it will close the case. A "notice of right to sue"—also referred to as a "right to sue letter"—will be issued to the charging party which authorizes them to file a lawsuit in court.

If the charge was filed against a state or local government employer under Title VII or the Americans with Disabilities Act, and the EEOC's investigation finds that there is reasonable cause to believe a violation of the law has occurred, and their conciliation efforts prove unsuccessful, the EEOC will then refer the charge to the Department of Justice. If the Department of Justice decides not to litigate the charge, a right to sue letter will be issued to the charging party, which entitles them to file his or her own lawsuit in court.

NOTICE OF RIGHT TO SUE

Issuing Agency

Except in cases where the charge has been dismissed, the Employment Litigation Section of the Department of Justice, through its right to sue unit, issues right to sue letters under Title VII and the Americans with Disabilities Act, on charges filed with the EEOC against state and local government employers or political subdivisions. The charging party may make a written request for a Notice of Right to Sue to the EEOC office where the charge is pending, or to the Department of Justice, Civil Rights Division, Employment Litigation Section, Right-to-Sue Unit, P.O. Box 65968, Washington, D.C. 20035-5968.

If the charge has been filed against a private employer or a union, only the EEOC has authority to issue a right to sue letter. Also, only the EEOC has authority to issue such a notice under the Age Discrimination in Employment Act of 1967, regardless of whether the respondent named in the charge is a state or local government employer or a private employer or a union.

Timetable for Issuing Notice

The EEOC must issue the Notice of Right to Sue 180 days after the Title VII charge has been filed, or when the EEOC concludes processing the case, whichever comes first. The EEOC may issue a Notice of Right to Sue at the request of a charging party prior to the expiration of the 180 day period provided the Director of the EEOC field office determines that the Commission will be unable to complete its administrative processing of the charge within 180 days from the filing of the charge. In that case, the Director must attach a written certificate to that effect to the Notice of Right to Sue pursuant to 29 C.F.R. §1601.28(a)(2).

Timetable for Initiating a Lawsuit

The charging party may file a lawsuit within 90 days after receiving the right to sue letter from the EEOC. Under Title VII and the ADA, if the EEOC does not issue the right to sue letter, a charging party can request that the EEOC issue the notice 180 days after the charge was first filed with the Commission, and may then bring suit within 90 days after receiving this notice.

The charging party should make sure they have legal representation in place because once the right to sue letter is issued, the time limitations for filing a lawsuit are strictly enforced. Attorney referrals may be obtained by contacting the local EEOC office, the courts, and the state or local bar association. It is important to retain an attorney who specializes in employment law. Individuals who cannot afford an attorney may contact the local legal aid office to find out whether they can handle the matter or refer it to another free or reduced cost legal services agency.

RESPONDING TO A CHARGE FILED WITH THE EEOC

The EEOC will notify the employer within 10 days after a charge of discrimination has been filed against them. Along with the notice, the EEOC will include a copy of the charge, which identifies the charging party and briefly sets forth the basis for the charge—e.g., sexual harassment—and the allegations. A plain language explanation of the EEOC charge process is generally included with the notice, as well as a cautionary statement concerning the non-retaliation provisions of the law.

Recordkeeping Obligation

The EEOC will also provide the employer with guidelines concerning the employer's obligation to retain records pertaining to the charge. Such records would include the employment records relating to the issues under investigation as a result of the charge. Once a charge is filed, these records must be kept until the final disposition of the charge or any lawsuit based on the charge.

Thus, when a charge is still not resolved after the EEOC investigation, and the charging party has received a notice of right to sue, "final disposition" means the date of expiration of the 90-day statutory period within which the aggrieved person may bring suit or, where suit is brought by the charging party or the EEOC, the date on which the litigation is terminated, including any appeals.

Investigation Procedure

The filing of a charge against an employer does not automatically mean that the government believes an act of discrimination has taken place. Under the law, when a charge of discrimination is made, the EEOC is obligated to investigate. If the EEOC believes the charge to be invalid based on its preliminary investigation, it will dismiss the case. If its preliminary investigation provides some reasonable cause to believe that discrimination has occurred, the investigation will continue.

During the investigation process, the employer will be asked to provide a response to the allegations in the charge, and furnish documents or information related to the EEOC investigation. The EEOC may also ask to visit the worksite and/or interview some of the charging party's coworkers.

It is to the employer's advantage to cooperate fully with the EEOC investigation, even if the employer believes the charge is frivolous or unfair. If the employer fails to do so, the EEOC will likely subpoena the information it requires from the employer, and note that the employer was uncooperative.

FILING A FEDERAL EMPLOYMENT DISCRIMINATION COMPLAINT

Employees or applicants who believe that they have been discriminated against by a federal agency have the right to file a complaint with that agency. The EEOC is responsible for enforcing the anti-discrimination laws in the federal sector. In addition to the right to file a discrimination claim on the basis of race, color, national origin, age, sex or disability, there are additional federal protections from discrimination on other bases. These include sexual orientation, status as a parent, marital status, political affiliation, and conduct that does not adversely affect the performance of the employee.

The EEOC conducts thousands of hearings every year for federal employees who have filed discrimination complaints. The EEOC also ensures that the federal departments and agencies maintain programs of equal employment opportunity required under federal law. However, as set forth below, the initial complaint of employment discrimination is not filed with the EEOC.

An employee who has a discrimination complaint against a department or agency of the federal government must first contact the authorized equal employment opportunity officer at the agency where the alleged discrimination took place. They must do so within 45 days of the discriminatory act.

The employee may elect to participate in counseling. In addition, the federal sector complaint processing regulations have been revised to require all federal agencies to establish alternative dispute resolution (ADR) programs. Ordinarily, counseling must be completed within 30 days, and ADR within 90 days. At the end of counseling, or if ADR is unsuccessful, the individual may then file a complaint with the particular agency.

The agency must acknowledge or reject the complaint. If the agency does not dismiss the complaint, it must conduct a complete and fair investigation within 180 days. At the conclusion of the investigation, the complainant may request either a hearing by an EEOC administrative judge, or an immediate final decision by the employing agency.

If the complainant elects a hearing, the EEOC judge must process the request for a hearing, issue findings of fact and conclusions of law, and order an appropriate remedy within 180 days. If the complainant elects to receive a final decision from the agency, the complainant may appeal an unfavorable decision—e.g., dismissal—to the EEOC within 30 days, or may file a lawsuit in U.S. District Court within 90 days.

If the complainant elects to file an appeal with the EEOC, the EEOC will examine the record and issue a decision. The EEOC may determine that the dismissal was improper, reverse the dismissal, and remand the matter back to the agency for completion of the investigation.

If the complaint involves a matter that is appealable to the Merit Systems Protection Board (MSPB)—e.g., a mixed case such as a termination of a career employee—the complainant may appeal the final agency decision to the MSPB within 20 days of receipt or file a lawsuit in the U.S. District Court within 30 days. The complainant may also petition the EEOC for review of the MSPB decision concerning the claim of discrimination.

The Administrative Grievance Procedure

Federal employees who believe they have been the victim of workplace harassment may also seek redress through the employing agency's administrative grievance procedure. Many agencies have their own grievance systems to resolve disputes between an employee and the agency that may not be heard elsewhere. In general, these systems try to achieve an informal resolution so that they do not have to be decided by higher levels of management. Specific procedures and time limitations vary from agency to agency.

An employee considering such a grievance must become familiar with the rules governing the particular agency's system. Employees should ask their human resource office for a copy of their agency grievance procedures to determine the subjects they cover and the procedures to follow.

The Negotiated Grievance Procedure

Federal employees who believe they have been the victim of workplace harassment may also wish to contact their union. Employees who are in a certified bargaining unit, that is, who are represented by a duly recognized labor organization and covered by a collective bargaining agreement, may file grievances in accordance with 5 U.S.C. § 7121. The definition of a grievance is contained in 5 U.S.C. § 7103(a)(9), but generally permits an employee to complain about most matters relating to employment. Unless specifically excluded from the grievance procedures by collective bargaining agreement, a grievance may allege the commission of a prohibited personnel practice.

As part of the negotiated grievance procedure, the union that represents the employee may elect to place the dispute before an arbitrator who is usually jointly selected by the union and the agency as provided in the collective bargaining agreement. The employee may not take the case to arbitration on their own.

Under current law, an arbitrator hearing a case concerning an alleged prohibited personnel practice may take the following action:

1. Stop any personnel action from taking place while he or she is hearing the case if the arbitrator determines that there are reasonable grounds to believe that a prohibited personnel practice has been committed or will be committed; or

2. Order the agency involved to take certain disciplinary action against the person committing the prohibited personnel practice.

The rules for appealing adverse arbitration decisions differ depending upon the subject of the grievance. Generally, matters that may be heard by the MSPB may be appealed to the United States Court of Appeals for the Federal Circuit. Otherwise, they may be appealed to the Federal Labor Relations Authority (FLRA).

The FLRA is an independent body that provides leadership in establishing policies and guidance relating to the Federal labor law. Among its functions is to receive and rule on "exceptions," that is, appeals from arbitral awards resulting from grievances. Ordinarily, however, one may not appeal a decision of the FLRA arising from arbitration to the courts.

CHAPTER 8:
PROTECTING YOUR RIGHTS

KEEP ACCURATE RECORDS

Preserving your rights in the workplace begins from the moment an individual is hired as an employee. Every employee should make it a practice to keep a personal employment file which documents their entire relationship with their employer. Although it is difficult to anticipate a problem in the workplace, it is much more difficult to prevail in a lawsuit if there is no documentation to support one's grievances.

EXAMPLE: After years of glowing performance evaluations, a female employee in a large chain store is suddenly fired after a new manager is put in charge of the department. The employee believes that she was fired because she refused to submit to the new manager's sexual advances—an unlawful motive for dismissal.

When asked why she was dismissed, the employee was told that she was incapable of meeting the requirements of the position—a position she has held for the past three years without incident. The employee points out that she received extremely high ratings on all of her past performance evaluations. The employee is told that there is no record of these evaluations in the employee's personnel folder. The employee's dismissal is upheld following the employer's internal complaint investigation.

The employee decides to file a workplace harassment charge with the EEOC against the employer. In support of her claim, she is asked to provide copies of her past performance evaluations. Unfortunately, the employee did not keep copies of any of these evaluations. The result—the employee has only her word against the employer to prove she was a highly capable worker, and that the stated reason for her dismissal was merely a pretext for the real motive—i.e., retaliation for rejecting the new manager's sexual overtures.

Because the employee did not keep a journal concerning the unlawful harassment, she may not recall when the incidents occurred, who was present who may have witnessed the incidents, and the specific comments or behavior of the manager.

Without corroboration from co-workers, and a clear recollection of the dates, times and circumstances surrounding the incidents, there is little to bolster this employee's claims. Often, co-workers do not want to get involved for fear that they will also lose their jobs. Again, it is her word against the manager.

If the employee had kept her performance evaluations for the past three years, it would certainly raise a valid question as to how the employee's evaluation could have plummeted so drastically after the new manager was hired.

In addition, if the employee had kept a journal detailing events which occurred at the workplace, there would be entries made concerning the date, time and witnesses to the manager's remarks or behavior. This would certainly weigh in favor of the employee's claim of harassment.

Therefore, one should not wait until a problem arises in the workplace to start accumulating evidence. All work-related documents, including employee handbooks, performance evaluations, and memorandums, etc., should be kept in the employee's personal employment file. In addition, it is advisable to keep a journal to document any unusual or significant events that occur in the workplace, including the basic facts, e.g., date, time, place, statements made, actions taken, and persons present, etc.

Problems which arise in the workplace do not always have to end up in litigation. Some problems can be worked out using informal methods. For example, the employee can try and work the problem out directly with the employer by arranging an informal meeting. Most employers would rather avoid having to answer an EEOC charge or defend a lawsuit if a legitimate grievance is brought to their attention. If the employee is a member of a union, the union representative may attend the meeting to help informally mediate any disputes.

In order to adequately prepare for this meeting, one must be knowledgeable about his or her legal rights concerning the specific problem, including the possible sanctions available to the employee under the law. The employee should calmly and intelligently set forth the basic facts surrounding the conflict, and explain how the employee's rights were thereby violated. This demonstrates to the employer that the employee is serious about pursuing legal action.

DEALING WITH THE SEXUAL HARASSER

As set forth in Chapter 3, sexual harassment is a type of workplace harassment that can both create a hostile work environment, and involve quid pro quo sexual demands. Victims of sexual harassment in the workplace must take immediate action to stop the behavior.

The first time the employee is subjected to behavior which may constitute sexual harassment, the employee must immediately state their objection to the behavior, whether it is a crude comment, sexual innuendo, or request for sexual favor. If possible, make the statement in the presence of others, in case you need a witness in the future. Taking a strong initial stance may stop the behavior from reoccurring without the need to go further.

Follow up with a written memo to the offender that you object to the particular behavior and request that it never happen again. You can also ask the personnel department to place a copy of the memo in the employment file of the offender, as well as in your own employment file. However, make sure you also keep a copy of the memo in your own personal employment file, which should be kept in your home. Unfortunately, documents have been known to "disappear" once a charge is filed or a lawsuit is initiated.

In addition to the memo, as set forth above, keep a journal with specific details of each incident. Document the time, place, date, objectionable behavior, and whether anyone was present. While your memory is fresh, write down what may have been said by the offender, and your response. Also keep a copy of your journal at home. In addition, keep copies of all document which can attest to the quality of your work, including performance evaluations, letters of commendation, etc.

Don't be afraid to share your experience with coworkers. There may be others who have been victimized by the individual, but have been too afraid or embarrassed to come forward. There is strength in numbers. An allegation of sexual harassment will be more believable if there are witnesses, particularly if those witnesses were also victims.

You should also prepare yourself financially in case your employer favors the side of the offender, particularly if the harasser is an important figure in the Company. Having money set aside in case you are fired, or if conditions at the workplace becomes too unbearable, will help you get through any periods of unemployment.

TAKING OFFICIAL ACTION AGAINST WORKPLACE HARASSMENT

If the harassment continues after the employee has asked that it stop, he or she must take some official action. Even though the employee is the victim of the harassment, there are steps he or she is required to take to try and avoid the harm and limit his or her injuries. For example, when faced with harassment in the workplace, the employee should follow the complaint procedures established by the employer.

Under the law, if the employee unreasonably fails to follow the employer's complaint procedures, the employer may not be responsible for the unlawful behavior, unless the harassment resulted in a tangible employment action. However, if the employee feared retaliation for following the employer's complaint procedure, this may be deemed a reasonable excuse for failing to do so. Nevertheless, the burden is on the employer to prove that the employee acted unreasonably under the circumstances.

Pending the employer's investigation, the employee may want to file a charge with the EEOC. However, it may be more prudent, unless there is a potential statute of limitations problem, to wait and see whether the employer is able to satisfactorily correct the situation.

If an individual believes he or she has been subjected to behaviors which are in violation of unlawful workplace harassment, and the employer's internal complaint procedure is ineffective, they should contact the Equal Employment Opportunity Commission (EEOC) to find out whether a charge may be filed. The EEOC covers workplace policy for employers with 15 or more employees. If you work for a smaller employee, state or local regulations may protect you. Federal employees should contact the Equal Opportunity office within their agency.

The deadline for filing an EEOC charge is either 180 or 300 days after the last date of alleged harassment, depending on the state in which the allegation arises. The fact that the employer is conducting an internal investigation does not stay—i.e., suspend or extend—the EEOC deadline.

As more fully discussed in Chapter 6, If the EEOC has determined that a violation has been committed, they will try to reach an agreement among the parties to resolve the charge. If they are unable to resolve the charge, they may refer the case to the Department of Justice for litigation, or may issue the victim a right to sue letter so that they can proceed with a civil action against the offender.

APPENDIX 1:
SELECTED PROVISIONS OF TITLE VII OF THE CIVIL RIGHTS ACT OF 1964

DEFINITIONS—SEC. 2000E. [SECTION 701]—[OMITTED]

EXEMPTION—SEC. 2000E-1. [SECTION 702]—[OMITTED]

UNLAWFUL EMPLOYMENT PRACTICES—SEC. 2000E-2. [SECTION 703]

(a) It shall be an unlawful employment practice for an employer—

(1) to fail or refuse to hire or to discharge any individual, or otherwise to discriminate against any individual with respect to his compensation, terms, conditions, or privileges of employment, because of such individual's race, color, religion, sex, or national origin; or

(2) to limit, segregate, or classify his employees or applicants for employment in any way which would deprive or tend to deprive any individual of employment opportunities or otherwise adversely affect his status as an employee, because of such individual's race, color, religion, sex, or national origin.

(b) It shall be an unlawful employment practice for an employment agency to fail or refuse to refer for employment, or otherwise to discriminate against, any individual because of his race, color, religion, sex, or national origin, or to classify or refer for employment any individual on the basis of his race, color, religion, sex, or national origin.

(c) It shall be an unlawful employment practice for a labor organization—

(1) to exclude or to expel from its membership, or otherwise to discriminate against, any individual because of his race, color, religion, sex, or national origin;

(2) to limit, segregate, or classify its membership or applicants for membership, or to classify or fail or refuse to refer for employment any individual, in any way which would deprive or tend to deprive any individual of employment opportunities, or would limit such employment opportunities or otherwise adversely affect his status as an employee or as an applicant for employment, because of such individual's race, color, religion, sex, or national origin; or

(3) to cause or attempt to cause an employer to discriminate against an individual in violation of this section.

(d) It shall be an unlawful employment practice for any employer, labor organization, or joint labor-management committee controlling apprenticeship or other training or retraining, including on-the-job training programs to discriminate against any individual because of his race, color, religion, sex, or national origin in admission to, or employment in, any program established to provide apprenticeship or other training.

(e) Notwithstanding any other provision of this subchapter, (1) it shall not be an unlawful employment practice for an employer to hire and employ employees, for an employment agency to classify, or refer for employment any individual, for a labor organization to classify its membership or to classify or refer for employment any individual, or for an employer, labor organization, or joint labor-management committee controlling apprenticeship or other training or retraining programs to admit or employ any individual in any such program, on the basis of his religion, sex, or national origin in those certain instances where religion, sex, or national origin is a bona fide occupational qualification reasonably necessary to the normal operation of that particular business or enterprise, and (2) it shall not be an unlawful employment practice for a school, college, university, or other educational institution or institution of learning to hire and employ employees of a particular religion if such school, college, university, or other educational institution or institution of learning is, in whole or in substantial part, owned, supported, controlled, or managed by a particular religion or by a particular religious corporation, association, or society, or if the curriculum of such school, college, university, or other educational institution or institution of learning is directed toward the propagation of a particular religion.

(f) As used in this subchapter, the phrase "unlawful employment practice" shall not be deemed to include any action or measure taken by an employer, labor organization, joint labor-management committee, or employment agency with respect to an individual who is a member of the Communist Party of the United States or of any other organization required to register as a Communist-action or Communist-front organization by final order of the Subversive Activities Control Board pursuant to the Subversive Activities Control Act of 1950 [50 U.S.C. 781 et seq.].

(g) Notwithstanding any other provision of this subchapter, it shall not be an unlawful employment practice for an employer to fail or refuse to hire and employ any individual for any position, for an employer to discharge any individual from any position, or for an employment agency to fail or refuse to refer any individual for employment in any position, or for a labor organization to fail or refuse to refer any individual for employment in any position, if—

(1) the occupancy of such position, or access to the premises in or upon which any part of the duties of such position is performed or is to be performed, is subject to any requirement imposed in the interest of the national security of the United States under any security program in effect pursuant to or administered under any statute of the United States or any Executive order of the President; and

(2) such individual has not fulfilled or has ceased to fulfill that requirement.

(h) Notwithstanding any other provision of this subchapter, it shall not be an unlawful employment practice for an employer to apply different standards of compensation, or different terms, conditions, or privileges of employment pursuant to a bona fide seniority or merit system, or a system which measures earnings by quantity or quality of production or to employees who work in different locations, provided that such differences are not the result of an intention to discriminate because of race, color, religion, sex, or national origin, nor shall it be an unlawful employment practice for an employer to give and to act upon the results of any professionally developed ability test provided that such test, its administration or action upon the results is not designed, intended or used to discriminate because of race, color, religion, sex or national origin. It shall not be an unlawful employment practice under this subchapter for any employer to differentiate upon the basis of sex in determining the amount of the wages or compensation paid or to be paid to employees of such employer if such differentiation is authorized by the provisions of section 206(d) of title 29 [section 6(d) of the Fair Labor Standards Act of 1938, as amended].

(i) Nothing contained in this subchapter shall apply to any business or enterprise on or near an Indian reservation with respect to any publicly announced employment practice of such business or enterprise under which a preferential treatment is given to any individual because he is an Indian living on or near a reservation.

(j) Nothing contained in this subchapter shall be interpreted to require any employer, employment agency, labor organization, or joint labor-management committee subject to this subchapter to grant preferential treatment to any individual or to any group because of the race, color, religion, sex, or national origin of such individual or group on account of an imbalance which may exist with respect to the total number or percentage of persons of any race, color, religion, sex, or national origin employed by any employer, referred or classified for employment by any employment agency or labor organization, admitted to membership or classified by any labor organization, or admitted to, or employed in, any apprenticeship or other training program, in comparison with the total number or percentage of persons of such race, color, religion, sex, or national origin in any community, State, section, or other area, or in the available work force in any community, State, section, or other area.

(k) (1) (A) An unlawful employment practice based on disparate impact is established under this title only if—

> (i) a complaining party demonstrates that a respondent uses a particular employment practice that causes a disparate impact on the basis of race, color, religion, sex, or national origin and the respondent fails to demonstrate that the challenged practice is job related for the position in question and consistent with business necessity; or

> (ii) the complaining party makes the demonstration described in subparagraph (C) with respect to an alternative employment practice and the respondent refuses to adopt such alternative employment practice.

(B) (i) With respect to demonstrating that a particular employment practice causes a disparate impact as described in subparagraph (A)(i), the complaining party shall demonstrate that each particular challenged employment practice causes a disparate impact, except that if the complaining party can demonstrate to the court that the elements of a respondent's decisionmaking process are not capable of separation for analysis, the decisionmaking process may be analyzed as one employment practice.

(B) (ii) If the respondent demonstrates that a specific employment practice does not cause the disparate impact, the respondent shall not be required to demonstrate that such practice is required by business necessity.

(C) The demonstration referred to by subparagraph (A)(ii) shall be in accordance with the law as it existed on June 4, 1989, with respect to the concept of `` alternative employment practice''.

(2) A demonstration that an employment practice is required by business necessity may not be used as a defense against a claim of intentional discrimination under this title.

(3) Notwithstanding any other provision of this title, a rule barring the employment of an individual who currently and knowingly uses or possesses a controlled substance, as defined in schedules I and II of section 102(6) of the Controlled Substances Act (21 U.S.C. 802(6)), other than the use or possession of a drug taken under the supervision of a licensed health care professional, or any other use or possession authorized by the Controlled Substances Act [21 U.S.C. 801 et seq.] or any other provision of Federal law, shall be considered an unlawful employment practice under this title only if such rule is adopted or applied with an intent to discriminate because of race, color, religion, sex, or national origin.

(l) It shall be an unlawful employment practice for a respondent, in connection with the selection or referral of applicants or candidates for employment or promotion, to adjust the scores of, use different cutoff scores for, or otherwise alter the results of, employment related tests on the basis of race, color, religion, sex, or national origin.

(m) Except as otherwise provided in this title, an unlawful employment practice is established when the complaining party demonstrates that race, color, religion, sex, or national origin was a motivating factor for any employment practice, even though other factors also motivated the practice.

(n) (1) (A) Notwithstanding any other provision of law, and except as provided in paragraph (2), an employment practice that implements and is within the scope of a litigated or consent judgment or order that resolves a claim of employment discrimination under the Constitution or Federal civil rights laws may not be challenged under the circumstances described in subparagraph (B).

(B) A practice described in subparagraph (A) may not be challenged in a claim under the Constitution or Federal civil rights laws—

(i) by a person who, prior to the entry of the judgment or order described in subparagraph (A), had—

(I) actual notice of the proposed judgment or order sufficient to apprise such person that such judgment or order might adversely affect the interests and legal rights of such person and that an opportunity was available to present objections to such judgment or order by a future date certain; and

(II) a reasonable opportunity to present objections to such judgment or order; or

(ii) by a person whose interests were adequately represented by another person who had previously challenged the judgment or order on the same legal grounds and with a similar factual situation, unless there has been an intervening change in law or fact.

(2) Nothing in this subsection shall be construed to—

(A) alter the standards for intervention under rule 24 of the Federal Rules of Civil Procedure or apply to the rights of parties who have successfully intervened pursuant to such rule in the proceeding in which the parties intervened;

(B) apply to the rights of parties to the action in which a litigated or consent judgment or order was entered, or of members of a class represented or sought to be represented in such action, or of members of a group on whose behalf relief was sought in such action by the Federal Government;

(C) prevent challenges to a litigated or consent judgment or order on the ground that such judgment or order was obtained through collusion or fraud, or is transparently invalid or was entered by a court lacking subject matter jurisdiction; or

(D) authorize or permit the denial to any person of the due process of law required by the Constitution.

(3) Any action not precluded under this subsection that challenges an employment consent judgment or order described in paragraph (1) shall be brought in the court, and if possible before the judge, that entered such judgment or order. Nothing in this subsection shall preclude a transfer of such action pursuant to section 1404 of title 28, United States Code.

OTHER UNLAWFUL EMPLOYMENT PRACTICES—SEC. 2000E-3. [SECTION 704]

(a) It shall be an unlawful employment practice for an employer to discriminate against any of his employees or applicants for employment, for an employment agency, or joint labor-management committee controlling apprenticeship or other training or retraining, including on-the-job training programs, to discriminate against any individual, or for a labor organization to discriminate against any member thereof or applicant for membership, because he has opposed any practice made an unlawful employment practice by this subchapter, or because he has made a charge, testified, assisted, or participated in any manner in an investigation, proceeding, or hearing under this subchapter.

(b) It shall be an unlawful employment practice for an employer, labor organization, employment agency, or joint labor-management committee controlling apprenticeship or other training or retraining, including on-the-job training programs, to print or publish or cause to be printed or published any notice or advertisement relating to employment by such an employer or membership in or any classification or referral for employment by such a labor organization, or relating to any classification or referral for employment by such an employment agency, or relating to admission to, or employment in, any program established to provide apprenticeship or other training by such a joint labor-management committee, indicating any preference, limitation, specification, or discrimination, based on race, color, religion, sex, or national origin, except that such a notice or advertisement may indicate a preference, limitation, specification, or discrimination based on religion, sex, or national origin when religion, sex, or national origin is a bona fide occupational qualification for employment.

EQUAL EMPLOYMENT OPPORTUNITY COMMISSION—SEC. 2000E-4. [SECTION 705]

(a) There is hereby created a Commission to be known as the Equal Employment Opportunity Commission, which shall be composed of five members, not more than three of whom shall be members of the same political party. Members of the Commission shall be appointed by the President by and with the advice and consent of the Senate for a term of five years. Any individual chosen to fill a vacancy shall be appointed only for the unexpired term of the member whom he shall succeed, and all members of the Commission shall continue to serve until their successors are appointed and qualified, except that no such member of the Commission shall continue to serve (1) for more than sixty days when the Congress is in session unless a nomination to fill such vacancy shall have been submitted to the Senate, or (2) after the adjournment sine die of the session of the Senate in which such nomination was submitted. The President shall designate one member to serve as Chairman of the Commission, and one member to serve as Vice Chairman. The Chairman shall be responsible on behalf of the Commission for the administrative operations of the Commission, and, except as provided in subsection (b) of this section, shall appoint, in accordance with the provisions of title 5 [United States Code] governing appointments in the competitive service, such officers, agents, attorneys, administrative law judges [hearing examiners], and employees as he deems necessary to assist it in the performance of its functions and to fix their compensation in accordance with the provisions of chapter 51 and subchapter III of chapter 53 of title 5 [United States Code], relating to classification and General Schedule pay rates: Provided, That assignment, removal, and compensation of administrative law judges [hearing examiners] shall be in accordance with sections 3105, 3344, 5372, and 7521 of title 5 [United States Code].

(b) (1) There shall be a General Counsel of the Commission appointed by the President, by and with the advice and consent of the Senate, for a term of four years. The General Counsel shall have responsibility for the conduct of litigation as provided in sections 2000e-5 and 2000e-6 of this title [sections 706 and 707]. The General Counsel shall have such other duties as the Commission may prescribe or as may be provided by law and shall concur with the Chairman of the Commission on the appointment and supervision of regional attorneys. The General Counsel of the Commission on the effective date of this Act shall continue in such position and perform the functions specified in this subsection until a successor is appointed and qualified.

(2) Attorneys appointed under this section may, at the direction of the Commission, appear for and represent the Commission in any case in court, provided that the Attorney General shall conduct all litigation to which the Commission is a party in the Supreme Court pursuant to this subchapter.

(c) A vacancy in the Commission shall not impair the right of the remaining members to exercise all the powers of the Commission and three members thereof shall constitute a quorum.

(d) The Commission shall have an official seal which shall be judicially noticed.

(e) The Commission shall at the close of each fiscal year report to the Congress and to the President concerning the action it has taken [the names, salaries, and duties of all individuals in its employ] and the moneys it has disbursed. It shall make such further reports on the cause of and means of eliminating discrimination and such recommendations for further legislation as may appear desirable.

(f) The principal office of the Commission shall be in or near the District of Columbia, but it may meet or exercise any or all its powers at any other place. The Commission may establish such regional or State offices as it deems necessary to accomplish the purpose of this subchapter.

(g) The Commission shall have power—

(1) to cooperate with and, with their consent, utilize regional, State, local, and other agencies, both public and private, and individuals;

(2) to pay to witnesses whose depositions are taken or who are summoned before the Commission or any of its agents the same witness and mileage fees as are paid to witnesses in the courts of the United States;

(3) to furnish to persons subject to this subchapter such technical assistance as they may request to further their compliance with this subchapter or an order issued thereunder;

(4) upon the request of (i) any employer, whose employees or some of them, or (ii) any labor organization, whose members or some of them, refuse or threaten to refuse to cooperate in effectuating the provisions of this subchapter, to assist in such effectuation by conciliation or such other remedial action as is provided by this subchapter;

(5) to make such technical studies as are appropriate to effectuate the purposes and policies of this subchapter and to make the results of such studies available to the public;

(6) to intervene in a civil action brought under section 2000e-5 of this title [section 706] by an aggrieved party against a respondent other than a government, governmental agency or political subdivision.

(h) (1) The Commission shall, in any of its educational or promotional activities, cooperate with other departments and agencies in the performance of such educational and promotional activities.

(2) In exercising its powers under this title, the Commission shall carry out educational and outreach activities (including dissemination of information in languages other than English) targeted to—

(A) individuals who historically have been victims of employment discrimination and have not been equitably served by the Commission; and

(B) individuals on whose behalf the Commission has authority to enforce any other law prohibiting employment discrimination, concerning rights and obligations under this title or such law, as the case may be.

(i) All officers, agents, attorneys, and employees of the Commission shall be subject to the provisions of section 7324 of title 5 [section 9 of the Act of August 2, 1939, as amended (the Hatch Act)], notwithstanding any exemption contained in such section.

(j) (1) The Commission shall establish a Technical Assistance Training Institute, through which the Commission shall provide technical assistance and training regarding the laws and regulations enforced by the Commission.

(2) An employer or other entity covered under this title shall not be excused from compliance with the requirements of this title because of any failure to receive technical assistance under this subsection.

(3) There are authorized to be appropriated to carry out this subsection such sums as may be necessary for fiscal year 1992.

ENFORCEMENT PROVISIONS—SEC. 2000E-5. [SECTION 706]

(a) The Commission is empowered, as hereinafter provided, to prevent any person from engaging in any unlawful employment practice as set forth in section 2000e-2 or 2000e-3 of this title [section 703 or 704].

(b) Whenever a charge is filed by or on behalf of a person claiming to be aggrieved, or by a member of the Commission, alleging that an employer, employment agency, labor organization, or joint labor-management committee controlling apprenticeship or other training or retraining, including on-the-job training programs, has engaged in an unlawful employment practice, the Commission shall serve a notice of the charge (including the date, place and circumstances of the alleged unlawful employment practice) on such employer, employment agency, labor organization, or joint labor-management committee (hereinafter referred to as the "respondent") within ten days, and shall make an investigation thereof. Charges shall be in writing under oath or affirmation and shall contain such information and be in such form as the Commission requires. Charges shall not be made public by the Commission. If the Commission determines after such investigation that there is not reasonable cause to believe that the charge is true, it shall dismiss the charge and promptly notify the person claiming to be aggrieved and the respondent of its action. In determining whether reasonable cause exists, the Commission shall accord substantial weight to final findings and orders made by State or local authorities in proceedings commenced under State or local law pursuant to the requirements of subsections (c) and (d) of this section. If the Commission determines after such investigation that there is reasonable cause to believe that the charge is true, the Commission shall endeavor to eliminate any such alleged unlawful employment practice by informal methods of conference, conciliation, and persuasion. Nothing said or done during and as a part of such informal endeavors may be made public by the Commission, its officers or employees, or used as evidence in a subsequent proceeding without the written consent of the persons concerned. Any person who makes public information in violation of this subsection shall be fined not more than $1,000 or imprisoned for not more than one year, or both. The Commission shall make its determination on reasonable cause as promptly as possible and, so far as practicable, not later than one hundred and twenty days from the filing of the charge or, where applicable under subsection (c) or (d) of this section, from the date upon which the Commission is authorized to take action with respect to the charge.

(c) In the case of an alleged unlawful employment practice occurring in a State, or political subdivision of a State, which has a State or local law prohibiting the unlawful employment practice alleged and establishing or authorizing a State or local authority to grant or seek relief from such practice or to institute criminal proceedings with respect thereto upon receiving notice thereof, no charge may be filed under subsection (a) of this section by the person aggrieved before the expiration of sixty days after proceedings have been commenced under the State or local law, unless such proceedings have been earlier terminated, provided that such sixty-day period shall be extended to one hundred and twenty days during the first year after the effective date of such State or local law. If any requirement for the commencement of such proceedings is imposed by a State or local authority other than a requirement of the filing of a written and signed statement of the facts upon which the proceeding is based, the proceeding shall be deemed to have been commenced for the purposes of this subsection at the time such statement is sent by registered mail to the appropriate State or local authority.

(d) In the case of any charge filed by a member of the Commission alleging an unlawful employment practice occurring in a State or political subdivision of a State which has a State or local law prohibiting the practice alleged and establishing or authorizing a State or local authority to grant or seek relief from such practice or to institute criminal proceedings with respect thereto upon receiving notice thereof, the Commission shall, before taking any action with respect to such charge, notify the appropriate State or local officials and, upon request, afford them a reasonable time, but not less than sixty days (provided that such sixty-day period shall be extended to one hundred and twenty days during the first year after the effective day of such State or local law), unless a shorter period is requested, to act under such State or local law to remedy the practice alleged.

(e) (1) A charge under this section shall be filed within one hundred and eighty days after the alleged unlawful employment practice occurred and notice of the charge (including the date, place and circumstances of the alleged unlawful employment practice) shall be served upon the person against whom such charge is made within ten days thereafter, except that in a case of an unlawful employment practice with respect to which the person aggrieved has initially instituted proceedings with a State or local agency with authority to grant or seek relief from such practice or to institute criminal proceedings with respect thereto upon receiving notice thereof, such charge shall be filed by or on behalf of the person aggrieved within three hundred days after the alleged unlawful employment practice occurred, or within thirty days after receiving notice that the State or local agency has terminated the proceedings under the State or local law, whichever is earlier, and a copy of such charge shall be filed by the Commission with the State or local agency.

(2) For purposes of this section, an unlawful employment practice occurs, with respect to a seniority system that has been adopted for an intentionally discriminatory purpose in violation of this title (whether or not that discriminatory purpose is apparent on the face of the seniority provision), when the seniority system is adopted, when an individual becomes subject to the seniority system, or when a person aggrieved is injured by the application of the seniority system or provision of the system.

(f) (1) If within thirty days after a charge is filed with the Commission or within thirty days after expiration of any period of reference under subsection (c) or (d) of this section, the Commission has been unable to secure from the respondent a conciliation agreement acceptable to the Commission, the Commission may bring a civil action against any respondent not a government, governmental agency, or political subdivision named in the charge. In the case of a respondent which is a government, governmental agency, or political subdivision, if the Commission has been unable to secure from the respondent a conciliation agreement acceptable to the Commission, the Commission shall take no further action and shall refer the case to the Attorney General who may bring a civil action against such respondent in the appropriate United States district court. The person or persons aggrieved shall have the right to intervene in a civil action brought by the Commission or the Attorney General in a case involving a government, governmental agency, or political subdivision. If a charge filed with the Commission pursuant to subsection (b) of this section, is dismissed by the Commission, or if within one hundred and eighty days from the filing of such charge or the expiration of any period of reference under subsection (c) or (d) of this section, whichever is later, the Commission has not filed a civil action under this section or the Attorney General has not filed a civil action in a case involving a government, governmental agency, or political subdivision, or the Commission has not entered into a conciliation agreement to which the person aggrieved is a party, the Commission, or the Attorney General in a case involving a government, governmental agency, or political subdivision, shall so notify the person aggrieved and within ninety days after the giving of such notice a civil action may be brought against the respondent named in the charge (A) by the person claiming to be aggrieved or (B) if such charge was filed by a member of the Commission, by any person whom the charge alleges was aggrieved by the alleged unlawful employment practice. Upon application by the complainant and in such circumstances as the court may deem just, the court may appoint an attorney for such complainant and may authorize the commencement of the action without the payment of fees, costs, or security. Upon timely application, the court may, in its discretion, permit the Commission, or the Attorney General in a case involving a government, governmental agency, or political subdivision, to intervene in such civil action upon certification that the case is of general public importance. Upon request, the court may, in its discretion, stay further proceedings for not more than sixty days pending the termination of State or local proceedings described in subsection (c) or (d) of this section or further efforts of the Commission to obtain voluntary compliance.

(2) Whenever a charge is filed with the Commission and the Commission concludes on the basis of a preliminary investigation that prompt judicial action is necessary to carry out the purposes of this Act, the Commission, or the Attorney General in a case involving a government, governmental agency, or political subdivision, may bring an action for appropriate temporary or preliminary relief pending final disposition of such charge. Any temporary restraining order or other order granting preliminary or temporary relief shall be issued in accordance with rule 65 of the Federal Rules of Civil Procedure. It shall be the duty of a court having jurisdiction over proceedings under this section to assign cases for hearing at the earliest practicable date and to cause such cases to be in every way expedited.

(3) Each United States district court and each United States court of a place subject to the jurisdiction of the United States shall have jurisdiction of actions brought under this subchapter. Such an action may be brought in any judicial district in the State in which the unlawful employment practice is alleged to have been committed, in the judicial district in which the employment records relevant to such practice are maintained and administered, or in the judicial district in which the aggrieved person would have worked but for the alleged unlawful employment practice, but if the respondent is not found within any such district, such an action may be brought within the judicial district in which

the respondent has his principal office. For purposes of sections 1404 and 1406 of title 28 [of the United States Code], the judicial district in which the respondent has his principal office shall in all cases be considered a district in which the action might have been brought.

(4) It shall be the duty of the chief judge of the district (or in his absence, the acting chief judge) in which the case is pending immediately to designate a judge in such district to hear and determine the case. In the event that no judge in the district is available to hear and determine the case, the chief judge of the district, or the acting chief judge, as the case may be, shall certify this fact to the chief judge of the circuit (or in his absence, the acting chief judge) who shall then designate a district or circuit judge of the circuit to hear and determine the case.

(5) It shall be the duty of the judge designated pursuant to this subsection to assign the case for hearing at the earliest practicable date and to cause the case to be in every way expedited. If such judge has not scheduled the case for trial within one hundred and twenty days after issue has been joined, that judge may appoint a master pursuant to rule 53 of the Federal Rules of Civil Procedure.

(g) (1) If the court finds that the respondent has intentionally engaged in or is intentionally engaging in an unlawful employment practice charged in the complaint, the court may enjoin the respondent from engaging in such unlawful employment practice, and order such affirmative action as may be appropriate, which may include, but is not limited to, reinstatement or hiring of employees, with or without back pay (payable by the employer, employment agency, or labor organization, as the case may be, responsible for the unlawful employment practice), or any other equitable relief as the court deems appropriate. Back pay liability shall not accrue from a date more than two years prior to the filing of a charge with the Commission. Interim earnings or amounts earnable with reasonable diligence by the person or persons discriminated against shall operate to reduce the back pay otherwise allowable.

(2) (A) No order of the court shall require the admission or reinstatement of an individual as a member of a union, or the hiring, reinstatement, or promotion of an individual as an employee, or the payment to him of any back pay, if such individual was refused admission, suspended, or expelled, or was refused employment or advancement or was suspended or discharged for any reason other than discrimination on account of race, color, religion, sex, or national origin or in violation of section 2000e-3(a) of this title [section 704(a)].

(B) On a claim in which an individual proves a violation under section 2000e-2(m) of this title [section 703(m)] and a respondent demonstrates that the respondent would have taken the same action in the absence of the impermissible motivating factor, the court—

(i) may grant declaratory relief, injunctive relief (except as provided in clause (ii)), and attorney's fees and costs demonstrated to be directly attributable only to the pursuit of a claim under section 2000e-2(m) of this title [section 703(m)]; and

(ii) shall not award damages or issue an order requiring any admission, reinstatement, hiring, promotion, or payment, described in subparagraph (A).

(h) The provisions of chapter 6 of title 29 [the Act entitled "An Act to amend the Judicial Code and to define and limit the jurisdiction of courts sitting in equity, and for other purposes," approved March 23, 1932 (29 U.S.C. 105-115)] shall not apply with respect to civil actions brought under this section.

(i) In any case in which an employer, employment agency, or labor organization fails to comply with an order of a court issued in a civil action brought under this section, the Commission may commence proceedings to compel compliance with such order.

(j) Any civil action brought under this section and any proceedings brought under subsection (i) of this section shall be subject to appeal as provided in sections 1291 and 1292, title 28 [United States Code].

(k) In any action or proceeding under this subchapter the court, in its discretion, may allow the prevailing party, other than the Commission or the United States, a reasonable attorney's fee (including expert fees) as part of the costs, and the Commission and the United States shall be liable for costs the same as a private person.

CIVIL ACTIONS BY THE ATTORNEY GENERAL—SEC. 2000E-6. [SECTION 707]—[OMITTED]

EFFECT ON STATE LAWS—SEC. 2000E-7. [SECTION 708]

Nothing in this subchapter shall be deemed to exempt or relieve any person from any liability, duty, penalty, or punishment provided by any present or future law of any State or political subdivision of a State, other than any such law which purports to require or permit the doing of any act which would be an unlawful employment practice under this subchapter.

INVESTIGATIONS, INSPECTIONS, RECORDS, STATE AGENCIES—SEC. 2000E-8. [SECTION 709]

(a) In connection with any investigation of a charge filed under section 2000e-5 of this title [section 706], the Commission or its designated representative shall at all reasonable times have access to, for the purposes of examination, and the right to copy any evidence of any person being investigated or proceeded against that relates to unlawful employment practices covered by this subchapter and is relevant to the charge under investigation.

(b) The Commission may cooperate with State and local agencies charged with the administration of State fair employment practices laws and, with the consent of such agencies, may, for the purpose of carrying out its functions and duties under this subchapter and within the limitation of funds appropriated specifically for such purpose, engage in and contribute to the cost of research and other projects of mutual interest undertaken by such agencies, and utilize the services of such agencies and their employees, and, notwithstanding any other provision of law, pay by advance or reimbursement such agencies and their employees for services rendered to assist the Commission in carrying out this subchapter. In furtherance of such cooperative efforts, the Commission may enter into written agreements with such State or local agencies and such agreements may include provisions under which the Commission shall refrain from processing a charge in any cases or class of cases specified in such agreements or under which the Commission shall relieve any person or class of persons in such State or locality from requirements imposed under this section. The Commission shall rescind any such agreement whenever it determines that the agreement no longer serves the interest of effective enforcement of this subchapter.

(c) Every employer, employment agency, and labor organization subject to this subchapter shall (1) make and keep such records relevant to the determinations of whether unlawful employment practices have been or are being committed, (2) preserve such records for such periods, and (3) make such reports therefrom as the Commission shall prescribe by regulation or order, after public hearing, as reasonable, necessary, or appropriate for the enforcement of this subchapter or the regulations or orders thereunder. The Commission shall, by regulation, require each employer, labor organization, and joint labor-management committee subject to this subchapter which controls an apprenticeship or other training program to maintain such records as are reasonably necessary to carry out the purposes of this subchapter, including, but not limited to, a list of applicants who wish to participate in such program, including the chronological order in which applications were received, and to furnish to the Commission upon request, a detailed description of the manner in which persons are selected to participate in the apprenticeship or other training program. Any employer, employment agency, labor organization, or joint labor-management committee which believes that the application to it of any regulation or order issued under this section would result in undue hardship may apply to the Commission for an exemption from the application of such regulation or order, and, if such application for an exemption is denied, bring a civil action in the United States district court for the district where such records are kept. If the Commission or the court, as the case may be, finds that the application of the regulation or order to the employer, employment agency, or labor organization in question would impose an undue hardship, the Commission or the court, as the case may be, may grant appropriate relief. If any person required to comply with the provisions of this subsection fails or refuses to do so, the United States district court for the district in which such person is found, resides, or transacts business, shall, upon application of the Commission, or the Attorney General in a case involving a government, governmental agency or political subdivision, have jurisdiction to issue to such person an order requiring him to comply.

(d) In prescribing requirements pursuant to subsection (c) of this section, the Commission shall consult with other interested State and Federal agencies and shall endeavor to coordinate its requirements with those adopted by such agencies. The Commission shall furnish upon request and without cost to any State or local agency charged with the administration of a fair employment practice law information obtained pursuant to subsection (c) of this section from any employer, employment agency, labor organization, or joint labor-management committee subject to the jurisdiction of such agency. Such information shall be furnished on condition that it not be made public by the recipient agency prior to the institution of a proceeding under State or local law involving such information. If this condition is violated by a recipient agency, the Commission may decline to honor subsequent requests pursuant to this subsection.

(e) It shall be unlawful for any officer or employee of the Commission to make public in any manner whatever any information obtained by the Commission pursuant to its authority under this section prior to the institution of any proceeding under this subchapter involving such information. Any officer or employee of the Commission who shall make public in any manner whatever any information in violation of this subsection shall be guilty, of a misdemeanor and upon conviction thereof, shall be fined not more than $1,000, or imprisoned not more than one year.

INVESTIGATORY POWERS—SEC. 2000E-9. [SECTION 710]

For the purpose of all hearings and investigations conducted by the Commission or its duly authorized agents or agencies, section 161 of title 29 [section 11 of the National Labor Relations Act] shall apply.

POSTING OF NOTICES; PENALTIES—SEC. 2000E-10. [SECTION 711]

(a) Every employer, employment agency, and labor organization, as the case may be, shall post and keep posted in conspicuous places upon its premises where notices to employees, applicants for employment, and members are customarily posted a notice to be prepared or approved by the Commission setting forth excerpts, from or, summaries of, the pertinent provisions of this subchapter and information pertinent to the filing of a complaint.

(b) A willful violation of this section shall be punishable by a fine of not more than $100 for each separate offense.

VETERANS' SPECIAL RIGHTS OR PREFERENCE— SEC. 2000E-11. [SECTION 712]

Nothing contained in this subchapter shall be construed to repeal or modify any Federal, State, territorial, or local law creating special rights or preference for veterans.

RULES AND REGULATIONS—SEC. 2000E-12. [SECTION 713]

(a) The Commission shall have authority from time to time to issue, amend, or rescind suitable procedural regulations to carry out the provisions of this subchapter. Regulations issued under this section shall be in conformity with the standards and limitations of subchapter II of chapter 5 of title 5 [the Administrative Procedure Act].

(b) In any action or proceeding based on any alleged unlawful employment practice, no person shall be subject to any liability or punishment for or on account of (1) the commission by such person of an unlawful employment practice if he pleads and proves that the act or omission complained of was in good faith, in conformity with, and in reliance on any written interpretation or opinion of the Commission, or (2) the failure of such person to publish and file any information required by any provision of this subchapter if he pleads and proves that he failed to publish and file such information in good faith, in conformity with the instructions of the Commission issued under this subchapter regarding the filing of such information. Such a defense, if established, shall be a bar to the action or proceeding, notwithstanding that (A) after such act or omission, such interpretation or opinion is modified or rescinded or is determined by judicial authority to be invalid or of no legal effect, or (B) after publishing or filing the description and annual reports, such publication or filing is determined by judicial authority not to be in conformity with the requirements of this subchapter.

FORCIBLY RESISTING THE COMMISSION OR ITS REPRESENTATIVES—SEC. 2000E-13. [SECTION 714]

The provisions of sections 111 and 1114, title 18 [United States Code], shall apply to officers, agents, and employees of the Commission in the performance of their official duties. Notwithstanding the provisions of sections 111 and 1114 of title 18 [United States Code], whoever in violation of the provisions of section 1114 of such title kills a person while engaged in or on account of the performance of his official functions under this Act shall be punished by imprisonment for any term of years or for life.

EQUAL EMPLOYMENT OPPORTUNITY COORDINATING COUNCIL—SEC. 2000E-14. [SECTION 715] [OMITTED]

EFFECTIVE DATE—SEC. 2000E-15. [SECTION 716]—[OMITTED]

EMPLOYMENT BY FEDERAL GOVERNMENT—SEC. 2000E-16. [SECTION 717]

(a) All personnel actions affecting employees or applicants for employment (except with regard to aliens employed outside the limits of the United States) in military departments as defined in section 102 of title 5 [United States Code], in executive agencies [other than the General Accounting Office] as defined in section 105 of title 5 [United States Code] (including employees and applicants for employment who are paid from nonappropriated funds), in the United States Postal Service and the Postal Rate Commission, in those units of the Government of the District of Columbia having positions in the competitive service, and in those units of the legislative and judicial branches of the Federal Government having positions in the competitive service, and in the Library of Congress shall be made free from any discrimination based on race, color, religion, sex, or national origin.

(b) Except as otherwise provided in this subsection, the Equal Employment Opportunity Commission [Civil Service Commission] shall have authority to enforce the provisions of subsection (a) of this section through appropriate remedies, including reinstatement or hiring of employees with or without back pay, as will effectuate the policies of this section, and shall issue such rules, regulations, orders and instructions as it deems necessary and appropriate to carry out its responsibilities under this section. The Equal Employment Opportunity Commission [Civil Service Commission] shall—

(1) be responsible for the annual review and approval of a national and regional equal employment opportunity plan which each department and agency and each appropriate unit referred to in subsection (a) of this section shall submit in order to maintain an affirmative program of equal employment opportunity for all such employees and applicants for employment;

(2) be responsible for the review and evaluation of the operation of all agency equal employment opportunity programs, periodically obtaining and publishing (on at least a semiannual basis) progress reports from each such department, agency, or unit; and

(3) consult with and solicit the recommendations of interested individuals, groups, and organizations relating to equal employment opportunity.

The head of each such department, agency, or unit shall comply with such rules, regulations, orders, and instructions which shall include a provision that an employee or applicant for employment shall be notified of any final action taken on any complaint of discrimination filed by him thereunder. The plan submitted by each department, agency, and unit shall include, but not be limited to—

(1) provision for the establishment of training and education programs designed to provide a maximum opportunity for employees to advance so as to perform at their highest potential; and

(2) a description of the qualifications in terms of training and experience relating to equal employment opportunity for the principal and operating officials of each such department, agency, or unit responsible for carrying out the equal employment opportunity program and of the allocation of personnel and resources proposed by such department, agency, or unit to carry out its equal employment opportunity program.

With respect to employment in the Library of Congress, authorities granted in this subsection to the Equal Employment Opportunity Commission [Civil Service Commission] shall be exercised by the Librarian of Congress.

(c) Within 90 days of receipt of notice of final action taken by a department, agency, or unit referred to in subsection (a) of this section, or by the Equal Employment Opportunity Commission [Civil Service Commission] upon an appeal from a decision or order of such department, agency, or unit on a complaint of discrimination based on race, color, religion, sex or national origin, brought pursuant to subsection (a) of this section, Executive Order 11478 or any succeeding Executive orders, or after one hundred and eighty days from the filing of the initial charge with the department, agency, or unit or with the Equal Employment Opportunity Commission [Civil Service Commission] on appeal from a decision or order of such department, agency, or unit until such time as final action may be taken by a department, agency, or unit, an employee or applicant for employment, if aggrieved by the final disposition of his complaint, or by the failure to take final action on his complaint, may file a civil action as provided in section 2000e-5 of this title [section 706], in which civil action the head of the department, agency, or unit, as appropriate, shall be the defendant.

(d) The provisions of section 2000e-5(f) through (k) of this title [section 706(f) through (k)], as applicable, shall govern civil actions brought hereunder, and the same interest to compensate for delay in payment shall be available as in cases involving nonpublic parties.

(e) Nothing contained in this Act shall relieve any Government agency or official of its or his primary responsibility to assure nondiscrimination in employment as required by the Constitution and statutes or of its or his responsibilities under Executive Order 11478 relating to equal employment opportunity in the Federal Government.

SPECIAL PROVISIONS WITH RESPECT TO DENIAL, TERMINATION, AND SUSPENSION OF GOVERNMENT CONTRACTS—SEC. 2000E-17. [SECTION 718] [OMITTED]

APPENDIX 2:
THE CIVIL RIGHTS ACT OF 1991

AN ACT

To amend the Civil Rights Act of 1964 to strengthen and improve Federal civil rights laws, to provide for damages in cases of intentional employment discrimination, to clarify provisions regarding disparate impact actions, and for other purposes.

Be it enacted by the Senate and House of Representatives of the United States of America in Congress assembled, This Act may be cited as the "Civil Rights Act of 1991".

FINDINGS—SEC. 2 [42 U.S.C. 1981 NOTE]

The Congress finds that—

(1) additional remedies under Federal law are needed to deter unlawful harassment and intentional discrimination in the workplace;

(2) the decision of the Supreme Court in Wards Cove Packing Co. v. Atonio, 490 U.S. 642 (1989) has weakened the scope and effectiveness of Federal civil rights protections; and

(3) legislation is necessary to provide additional protections against unlawful discrimination in employment.

PURPOSES—SEC. 3 [42 U.S.C. 1981 NOTE]

The purposes of this Act are—

(1) to provide appropriate remedies for intentional discrimination and unlawful harassment in the workplace;

(2) to codify the concepts of "business necessity" and "job related" enunciated by the Supreme Court in Griggs v. Duke Power Co., 401 U.S. 424 (1971), and in the other Supreme Court decisions prior to Wards Cove Packing Co. v. Atonio, 490 U.S. 642 (1989);

(3) to confirm statutory authority and provide statutory guidelines for the adjudication of disparate impact suits under title VII of the Civil Rights Act of 1964 (42 U.S.C. 2000e et seq.); and

(4) to respond to recent decisions of the Supreme Court by expanding the scope of relevant civil rights statutes in order to provide adequate protection to victims of discrimination.

TITLE I—FEDERAL CIVIL RIGHTS REMEDIES

PROHIBITION AGAINST ALL RACIAL DISCRIMINATION IN THE MAKING AND ENFORCEMENT OF CONTRACTS—SEC. 101

Section 1977 of the Revised Statutes (42 U.S.C. 1981) is amended—

(1) by inserting "(a)" before "All persons within"; and

(2) by adding at the end the following new subsections:

"(b) For purposes of this section, the term 'make and enforce contracts' includes the making, performance, modification, and termination of contracts, and the enjoyment of all benefits, privileges, terms, and conditions of the contractual relationship.

"(c) The rights protected by this section are protected against impairment by nongovernmental discrimination and impairment under color of State law."

DAMAGES IN CASES OF INTENTIONAL DISCRIMINATION—SEC. 102

The Revised Statutes are amended by inserting after section 1977 (42 U.S.C. 1981) the following new section:

"SEC. 1977A. DAMAGES IN CASES OF INTENTIONAL DISCRIMINATION IN EMPLOYMENT. [42 U.S.C. 1981a]

"(a) Right of Recovery.—

"(1) Civil Rights.—In an action brought by a complaining party under section 706 or 717 of the Civil Rights Act of 1964 (42 U.S.C. 2000e-5) against a respondent who engaged in unlawful intentional discrimination (not an employment practice that is unlawful because of its disparate impact) prohibited under section 703, 704, or 717 of the Act (42 U.S.C. 2000e-2 or 2000e-3), and provided that the complaining party cannot recover under section 1977 of the Revised Statutes (42 U.S.C. 1981), the complaining party may recover compensatory and punitive damages as allowed in subsection (b), in addition to any relief authorized by section 706(g) of the Civil Rights Act of 1964, from the respondent.

"(2) Disability.—In an action brought by a complaining party under the powers, remedies, and procedures set forth in section 706 or 717 of the Civil Rights Act of 1964 (as provided in section 107(a) of the Americans with Disabilities Act of 1990 (42 U.S.C. 12117 (a)), and section 505(a)(1) of the Rehabilitation Act of 1973 (29 U.S.C. 794a(a)(1)), respectively) against a respondent who engaged in unlawful intentional discrimination (not an employment practice that is unlawful because of its disparate impact) under section 501 of the Rehabilitation Act of 1973 (29 U.S.C. 791) and the regulations implementing section 501, or who violated the requirements of section 501 of the Act or the regulations implementing section 501 concerning the provision of a reasonable accommodation, or section 102 of the Americans with Disabilities Act of 1990 (42 U.S.C. 12112), or committed a violation of section 102(b)(5) of the Act, against an individual, the complaining party may recover compensatory and punitive damages as allowed in subsection (b), in addition to any relief authorized by section 706(g) of the Civil Rights Act of 1964, from the respondent.

"(3) Reasonable Accommodation and Good Faith Effort.—In cases where a discriminatory practice involves the provision of a reasonable accommodation pursuant to section 102(b)(5) of the Americans with Disabilities Act of 1990 or regulations implementing section 501 of the Rehabilitation Act of 1973, damages may not be awarded under this section where the covered entity demonstrates good faith efforts, in consultation with the person with the disability who has informed the covered entity that accommodation is needed, to identify and make a reasonable accommodation that would provide such individual with an equally effective opportunity and would not cause an undue hardship on the operation of the business.

"(b) Compensatory and Punitive Damages.—

"(1) Determination of punitive damages.—A complaining party may recover punitive damages under this section against a respondent (other than a government, government agency or political subdivision) if the complaining party demonstrates that the respondent engaged in a discriminatory practice or discriminatory practices with malice or with reckless indifference to the federally protected rights of an aggrieved individual.

"(2) Exclusions from compensatory damages.—Compensatory damages awarded under this section shall not include backpay, interest on backpay, or any other type of relief authorized under section 706(g) of the Civil Rights Act of 1964.

"(3) Limitations.—The sum of the amount of compensatory damages awarded under this section for future pecuniary losses, emotional pain, suffering, inconvenience, mental anguish, loss of enjoyment of life, and other nonpecuniary losses, and the amount of punitive damages awarded under this section, shall not exceed, for each complaining party—

"(A) in the case of a respondent who has more than 14 and fewer than 101 employees in each of 20 or more calendar weeks in the current or preceding calendar year, $50,000;

"(B) in the case of a respondent who has more than 100 and fewer than 201 employees in each of 20 or more calendar weeks in the current or preceding calendar year, $100,000; and

"(C) in the case of a respondent who has more than 200 and fewer than 501 employees in each of 20 or more calendar weeks in the current or preceding calendar year, $200,000; and

"(D) in the case of a respondent who has more than 500 employees in each of 20 or more calendar weeks in the current or preceding calendar year, $300,000.

"(4) Construction.—Nothing in this section shall be construed to limit the scope of, or the relief available under, section 1977 of the Revised Statutes (42 U.S.C. 1981).

"(c) Jury Trial.—If a complaining party seeks compensatory or punitive damages under this section—

"(1) any party may demand a trial by jury; and

"(2) the court shall not inform the jury of the limitations described in subsection (b)(3).

"(d) Definitions.—As used in this section:

"(1) Complaining party.—The term 'complaining party' means—

"(A) in the case of a person seeking to bring an action under subsection (a)(1), the Equal Employment Opportunity Commission, the Attorney General, or a person who may bring an action or proceeding under title VII of the Civil Rights Act of 1964 (42 U.S.C. 2000e et seq.); or

"(B) in the case of a person seeking to bring an action under subsection (a)(2), the Equal Employment Opportunity Commission, the Attorney General, a person who may bring an action or proceeding under section 505(a)(1) of the Rehabilitation Act of 1973 (29 U.S.C. 794a(a)(1)), or a person who may bring an action or proceeding under title I of the Americans with Disabilities Act of 1990 (42 U.S.C. 12101 et seq.).

"(2) Discriminatory practice.—The term 'discriminatory practice' means the discrimination described in paragraph (1), or the discrimination or the violation described in paragraph (2), of subsection (a)."

ATTORNEY'S FEES—SEC. 103

[This section amends section 722 of the Revised Statutes (42 U.S.C. 1988) by adding a reference to section 102 of the Civil Rights Act of 1991 to the list of civil rights actions in which reasonable attorney's fees may be awarded to the prevailing party, other than the United States.]

The last sentence of section 722 of the Revised Statutes (42 U.S.C. 1988) is amended by inserting ",1977A" after "1977".

DEFINITIONS—SEC. 104

[This section amends section 701 of the Civil Rights Act of 1964 (42 U.S.C. 2000e) by adding the following new subsections: (l) "complaining party," (m) "demonstrates," and (n) "respondent".]

BURDEN OF PROOF IN DISPARATE IMPACT CASES—SEC. 105

(a) [This subsection amends section 703 of the Civil Rights Act of 1964 (42 U.S.C. 2000e-2) by adding a new subsection (k), on the burden of proof in disparate impact cases.]

(b) No statements other than the interpretive memorandum appearing at Vol. 137 Congressional Record S 15276 (daily ed. Oct. 25, 1991) shall be considered legislative history of, or relied upon in any way as legislative history in construing or applying, any provision of this Act that relates to Wards Cove—Business necessity/cumulation/alternative business practice. [42 U.S.C. 1981 note]

PROHIBITION AGAINST DISCRIMINATORY USE OF TEST SCORES—SEC. 106

[This section amends section 703 of the Civil Rights Act of 1964 (42 U.S.C. 2000e-2) by adding a new subsection (l), on the prohibition against discriminatory use of test scores.]

CLARIFYING PROHIBITION AGAINST IMPERMISSIBLE CONSIDERATION OF RACE, COLOR, RELIGION, SEX, OR NATIONAL ORIGIN IN EMPLOYMENT PRACTICES—SEC. 107

(a) In general. [This subsection amends section 703 of the Civil Rights Act of 1964 (42 U.S.C. 2000e-2) by adding a new subsection (m), clarifying the prohibition against consideration of race, color, religion, sex, or national origin in employment practices.]

(b) Enforcement provisions. [This subsection amends section 706(g) of the Civil Rights Act of 1964 (42 U.S.C. 2000e-5(g)) by renumbering existing subsection (g), and adding at the end a new subparagraph (B) to provide a limitation on available relief in "mixed motive" cases (where the employer demonstrates it would have made the same decision in the absence of discrimination).]

FACILITATING PROMPT AND ORDERLY RESOLUTION OF CHALLENGES TO EMPLOYMENT PRACTICES IMPLEMENTING LITIGATED OR CONSENT JUDGMENTS OR ORDERS—SEC. 108

[This section amends section 703 of the Civil Rights Act of 1964 (42 U.S.C. 2000e-2) by adding a new subsection (n), on the resolution of challenges to employment practices implementing litigated or consent judgments or orders.]

PROTECTION OF EXTRATERRITORIAL EMPLOYMENT—SEC. 109

(a) Definition of Employee. [This subsection amends the definition of "employee" in section 701(f) of the Civil Rights Act of 1964 (42 U.S.C. 2000e(f)) and section 101(4) of the Americans with Disabilities Act of 1990 (42 U.S.C. 12111(4)) by adding a sentence to the end of each definition to include U.S. citizens employed abroad within the laws' protections.]

(b) Exemption. [This subsection amends section 702 of the Civil Rights Act of 1964 (42 U.S.C. 2000e-1) by adding new subsections (b) (on compliance with the statute if violative of foreign law) and (c) (on the control of a corporation incorporated in a foreign country). This subsection similarly amends section 102 of the Americans with Disabilities Act of 1990 (42 U.S.C. 12112) by relettering the existing subsections and adding a new subsection (c) "Covered Entities in Foreign Countries."]

(c) Application of Amendments.—The amendments made by this section shall not apply with respect to conduct occurring before the date of the enactment of this Act. [42 U.S.C. 2000e note]

TECHNICAL ASSISTANCE TRAINING INSTITUTE—SEC. 110

(a) Technical Assistance. [This subsection amends section 705 of the Civil Rights Act of 1964 (42 U.S.C. 2000e-4) by adding a new subsection (j), establishing the Technical Assistance Training Institute.]

(b) Effective Date.—The amendment made by this section shall take effect on the date of enactment of this Act. [42 U.S.C. 2000e-4 note]

EDUCATION AND OUTREACH—SEC. 111

[This section amends section 705(h) of the Civil Rights Act of 1964 (42 U.S.C. 2000e-4(h)) by renumbering the existing subsection and adding at the end a paragraph requiring the EEOC to engage in certain educational and outreach activities.]

EXPANSION OF RIGHT TO CHALLENGE DISCRIMINATORY SENIORITY SYSTEMS—SEC. 112

[This section amends section 706(e) of the Civil Rights Act of 1964 (42 U.S.C. 2000e-5(e)) by renumbering the subsection and adding at the end a paragraph to expand the right of claimants to challenge discriminatory seniority systems.]

AUTHORIZING AWARD OF EXPERT FEES—SEC. 113

(a) Revised Statutes.—Section 722 of the Revised Statutes is amended-

(1) by designating the first and second sentences as subsections (a) and (b), respectively, and indenting accordingly; and

(2) by adding at the end the following new subsection:

"(c) In awarding an attorney's fee under subsection (b) in any action or proceeding to enforce a provision of section 1977 or 1977A of the Revised Statutes, the court, in its discretion, may include expert fees as part of the attorney's fee." [42 U.S.C. 1988]

(b) Civil Rights Act of 1964. [This section amends section 706(k) of the Civil Rights Act of 1964 (42 U.S.C. 2000e-5(k)) to provide for recovery of expert fees as part of an attorney's fees award.]

PROVIDING FOR INTEREST AND EXTENDING THE STATUTE OF LIMITATIONS IN ACTIONS AGAINST THE FEDERAL GOVERNMENT—SEC. 114

[This section amends section 717 of the Civil Rights Act of 1964 (42 U.S.C. 2000e-16) by extending the time for federal employees or applicants to file a civil action from 30 to 90 days (from receipt of notice of final action taken by a department, agency or unit), and allowing federal employees or applicants the same interest to compensate for delay in payments as is available in cases involving nonpublic parties.]

NOTICE OF LIMITATIONS PERIOD UNDER THE AGE DISCRIMINATION IN EMPLOYMENT ACT OF 1967—SEC. 115

[This section amends section 7(e) of the Age Discrimination in Employment Act of 1967 (ADEA) (29 U.S.C. 626(e)) by eliminating the two- and three-year statute of limitations and making ADEA suit- filing requirements the same as those under Title VII, and requiring the EEOC to provide notice to charging parties upon termination of the proceedings.]

LAWFUL, COURT-ORDERED REMEDIES, AFFIRMATIVE ACTION, AND CONCILIATION AGREEMENTS NOT AFFECTED—SEC. 116 [42 U.S.C. 1981 note]

Nothing in the amendments made by this title shall be construed to affect court-ordered remedies, affirmative action, or conciliation agreements, that are in accordance with the law.

COVERAGE OF HOUSE OF REPRESENTATIVES AND THE AGENCIES OF THE LEGISLATIVE BRANCH—SEC. 117

(a) Coverage of the House of Representatives. [This subsection extends the rights and protections of Title VII of the Civil Rights Act of 1964, as amended, to employees of the U.S. House of Representatives. Procedures for processing discrimination complaints are handled internally by the House, not by the EEOC.] [2 U.S.C. 601]

(b) Instrumentalities of Congress. [This subsection extends the rights and protections of the Civil Rights Act of 1991 and Title VII of the Civil Rights Act of 1964, as amended, to "Instrumentalities of Congress," which are defined to include: the Architect of the Capitol, the Congressional Budget Office, the General Accounting Office, the Government Printing Office, the Office of Technology Assessment, and the United States Botanic Garden. Each agency is to establish its own remedies and procedures for enforcement.]

ALTERNATIVE MEANS OF DISPUTE RESOLUTION—SEC. 118 [42 U.S:C. 1981 note]

Where appropriate and to the extent authorized by law, the use of alternative means of dispute resolution, including settlement negotiations, conciliation, facilitation, mediation, factfinding, minitrials, and arbitration, is encouraged to resolve disputes arising under the Acts or provisions of Federal law amended by this title.

TITLE II—GLASS CEILING

[This title sets up a "Glass Ceiling Commission" to focus attention on, and complete a study relating to, the existence of artificial barriers to the advancement of women and minorities in the workplace, and to make recommendations for overcoming such barriers. The Commission is to be composed of 21 members, with the Secretary of Labor serving as the Chairperson of the Commission. This title does not directly impose any responsibilities or obligations on the EEOC except to provide information and technical assistance as requested by the new Commission.] [42 U.S.C. 2000e note]

TITLE III—GOVERNMENT EMPLOYEE RIGHTS ACT OF 1991—SEC. 301 [2 U.S.C. 1201]

(a) Short title.—This title may be cited as the "Government Employee Rights Act of 1991".

(b) Purpose.—The purpose of this title is to provide procedures to protect the right of Senate and other government employees, with respect to their public employment, to be free of discrimination on the basis of race, color, religion, sex, national origin, age, or disability.

(c) Definitions.—For purposes of this title:

(1) Senate employee.—The term "Senate employee" or "employee" means—

(A) any employee whose pay is disbursed by the Secretary of the Senate;

(B) any employee of the Architect of the Capitol who is assigned to the Senate Restaurants or to the Superintendent of the Senate Office Buildings;

(C) any applicant for a position that will last 90 days or more and that is to be occupied by an individual described in subparagraph (A) or (B); or

(D) any individual who was formerly an employee described in subparagraph (A) or (B) and whose claim of a violation arises out of the individual's Senate employment.

(2) Head of employing office.—The term "head of employing office" means the individual who has final authority to appoint, hire, discharge, and set the terms, conditions or privileges of the Senate employment of an employee.

(3) Violation.—The term "violation" means a practice that violates section 302 of this title.

DISCRIMINATORY PRACTICES PROHIBITED—SEC. 302 [2 U.S.C. 1202]

[Sections 320 and 321 (which protect Presidential appointees and previously exempt state employees who may file complaints of discrimination with EEOC under this title) refer to the rights, protections and remedies of this section and section 307(h).]

All personnel actions affecting employees of the Senate shall be made free from any discrimination based on—

(1) race, color, religion, sex, or national origin, within the meaning of section 717 of the Civil Rights Act of 1964 (42 U.S.C. 2000e-16);

(2) age, within the meaning of section 15 of the Age Discrimination in Employment Act of 1967 (29 U.S.C. 633a); or

(3) handicap or disability, within the meaning of section 501 of the Rehabilitation Act of 1973 (29 U.S.C. 791) and sections 102-104 of the Americans with Disabilities Act of 1990 (42 U.S.C. 12112-14).

[SECTIONS 303 THROUGH 306: Section 303 (2 U.S.C. 1203) establishes the Office of Senate Fair Employment Practices, which will administer the procedures set forth in sections 304 through 307. Section 304 (2 U.S.C. 1204) outlines the four-step procedure described in Sections 305 through 309 for consideration of alleged violations. Section 305 (2 U.S.C. 1205) describes the Step I counseling procedures. Section 306 (2 U.S.C. 1206) describes the Step II mediation process. Section 307 (2 U.S.C. 1207), described fully below, sets forth the formal complaint and hearing procedures.]

STEP III: FORMAL COMPLAINT AND HEARING—SEC. 307 [2 U.S.C. 1207]

[SECTION 307, SUBSECTIONS (a) THROUGH (g), AND (i): Subsections (a) through (g), and (i) of Section 307 describe the process from the formal complaint through the hearing stage.]

[Sections 320 and 321 (which protect Presidential appointees and previously exempt state employees who may file complaints of discrimination with EEOC under this title) refer to the rights, protections and remedies of section 302 and the following subsection.]

(h) Remedies.—If the hearing board determines that a violation has occurred, it shall order such remedies as would be appropriate if awarded under section 706 (g) and (k) of the Civil Rights Act of 1964 (42 U.S.C. 2000e-5 (g) and (k)), and may also order the award of such compensatory damages as would be appropriate if awarded under section 1977 and section 1977A (a) and (b)(2) of the Revised Statutes (42 U.S.C. 1981 and 1981A (a) and (b)(2)). In the case of a determination that a violation based on age has occurred, the hearing board shall order such remedies as would be appropriate if awarded under section 15(c) of the Age Discrimination in Employment Act of 1967 (29 U.S.C. 633a(c)). Any order requiring the payment of money must be approved by a Senate resolution reported by the Committee on Rules and Administration. The hearing board shall have no authority to award punitive damages.

[SECTIONS 308 THROUGH 313: Section 308 (2 U.S.C. 1208) describes the procedures by which a Senate employee or head of an employing office may request a review by the Select Committee on Ethics of a decision issued under Section 307. Section 309 (2 U.S.C. 1209) describes the circumstances under which a Senate employee or Member of the Senate may petition for a review by the United States Court of Appeals for the Federal Circuit. Section 310 (2 U.S.C. 1210) describes the procedures by which a complaint may be resolved. Section 311 (2 U.S.C. 1211) enumerates reimbursable costs of attending hearings. Section 312 (2 U.S.C. 1212) prohibits intimidation or reprisal against any employee because of the exercise of a right under this title. Section 313 (2 U.S.C. 1213) outlines confidentiality requirements for counseling, mediation, hearings, final decisions, and records.]

EXERCISE OF RULEMAKING POWER—SEC. 314 [2 U.S.C. 1214]

The provisions of this title, except for sections 309, 320, 321, and 322, are enacted by the Senate as an exercise of the rulemaking power of the Senate, with full recognition of the right of the Senate to change its rules, in the same manner, and to the same extent, as in the case of any other rule of the Senate. Notwithstanding any other provision of law, except as provided in section 309, enforcement and adjudication with respect to the discriminatory practices prohibited by section 302, and arising out of Senate employment, shall be within the exclusive jurisdiction of the United States Senate.

TECHNICAL AND CONFORMING AMENDMENTS—SEC. 315

[This section makes technical and conforming amendments to section 509 of the Americans with Disabilities Act of 1990 (ADA) (42 U.S.C. 12209) with respect to Senate employees.]

[SECTIONS 316 THROUGH 319: Section 316 (2 U.S.C. 1215) states that the consideration of political affiliation, domicile, and political compatibility with the employing office in an employment decision shall not be considered a violation of this title. Section 317 (2 U.S.C. 1216) states that a Senate employee may not commence a judicial proceeding to redress a prohibited discriminatory practice, except as provided in this title. Sec. 318 (2 U.S.C. 1217) expresses the Senate's view that legislation should be enacted to provide the same or comparable rights and remedies as are provided under this title to Congressional employees lacking such rights and remedies. Section 319 (2 U.S.C. 1218) reaffirms the Senate's commitment to Rule XLII of the Standing Rules of the Senate.]

COVERAGE OF PRESIDENTIAL APPOINTEES—SEC. 320 [2 U.S.C. 1219]

(a) In General.—

(1) Application.—The rights, protections, and remedies provided pursuant to section 302 and 307(h) of this title shall apply with respect to employment of Presidential appointees.

(2) Enforcement by administrative action.—Any Presidential appointee may file a complaint alleging a violation, not later than 180 days after the occurrence of the alleged violation, with the Equal Employment Opportunity Commission, or such other entity as is designated by the President by Executive Order, which, in accordance with the principles and procedures set forth in sections 554 through 557 of title 5, United States Code, shall determine whether a violation has occurred and shall set forth its determination in a final order. If the Equal Employment Opportunity Commission, or such other entity as is designated by the President pursuant to this section, determines that a violation has occurred, the final order shall also provide for appropriate relief.

(3) Judicial review.—

(A) In general.—Any party aggrieved by a final order under paragraph (2) may petition for review by the United States Court of Appeals for the Federal Circuit.

(B) Law applicable.—Chapter 158 of title 28, United States Code, shall apply to a review under this section except that the Equal Employment Opportunity Commission or such other entity as the President may designate under paragraph (2) shall be an "agency" as that term is used in chapter 158 of title 28, United States Code.

(C) Standard of review.—To the extent necessary to decision and when presented, the reviewing court shall decide all relevant questions of law and interpret constitutional and statutory provisions. The court shall set aside a final order under paragraph (2) if it is determined that the order was—

(i) arbitrary, capricious, an abuse of discretion, or otherwise not consistent with law;

(ii) not made consistent with required procedures; or

(iii) unsupported by substantial evidence.

In making the foregoing determinations, the court shall review the whole record or those parts of it cited by a party, and due account shall be taken of the rule of prejudicial error.

(D) Attorney's fees.—If the presidential appointee is the prevailing party in a proceeding under this section, attorney's fees may be allowed by the court in accordance with the standards prescribed under section 706(k) of the Civil Rights Act of 1964 (42 U.S.C. 2000e-5(k)).

(b) Presidential appointee.—For purposes of this section, the term "Presidential appointee" means any officer or employee, or an applicant seeking to become an officer or employee, in any unit of the Executive Branch, including the Executive Office of the President, whether appointed by the President or by any other appointing authority in the Executive Branch, who is not already entitled to bring an action under any of the statutes referred to in section 302 but does not include any individual—

(1) whose appointment is made by and with the advice and consent of the Senate;

(2) who is appointed to an advisory committee, as defined in section 3(2) of the Federal Advisory Committee Act (5 U.S.C. App.); or

(3) who is a member of the uniformed services.

COVERAGE OF PREVIOUSLY EXEMPT STATE EMPLOYEES—SEC. 321 [2 U.S.C. 1220]

(a) Application.—The rights, protections, and remedies provided pursuant to section 302 and 307(h) of this title shall apply with respect to employment of any individual chosen or appointed, by a person elected to public office in any State or political subdivision of any State by the qualified voters thereof—

(1) to be a member of the elected official's personal staff;

(2) to serve the elected official on the policymaking level; or

(3) to serve the elected official as an immediate advisor with respect to the exercise of the constitutional or legal powers of the office.

(b) Enforcement by administrative action.—

(1) In general.—Any individual referred to in subsection (a) may file a complaint alleging a violation, not later than 180 days after the occurrence of the alleged violation, with the Equal Employment Opportunity Commission, which, in accordance with the principles and procedures set forth in sections 554 through 557 of title 5, United

States Code, shall determine whether a violation has occurred and shall set forth its determination in a final order. If the Equal Employment Opportunity Commission determines that a violation has occurred, the final order shall also provide for appropriate relief.

(2) Referral to state and local authorities.—

(A) Application.—Section 706(d) of the Civil Rights Act of 1964 (42 U.S.C. 2000e-5(d)) shall apply with respect to any proceeding under this section.

(B) Definition.—For purposes of the application described in subparagraph (A), the term "any charge filed by a member of the Commission alleging an unlawful employment practice" means a complaint filed under this section.

(c) Judicial review.—Any party aggrieved by a final order under subsection (b) may obtain a review of such order under chapter 158 of title 28, United States Code. For the purpose of this review, the Equal Employment Opportunity Commission shall be an "agency" as that term is used in chapter 158 of title 28, United States Code.

(d) Standard of review.—To the extent necessary to decision and when presented, the reviewing court shall decide all relevant questions of law and interpret constitutional and statutory provisions. The court shall set aside a final order under subsection (b) if it is determined that the order was—

(1) arbitrary, capricious, an abuse of discretion, or otherwise not consistent with law;

(2) not made consistent with required procedures; or

(3) unsupported by substantial evidence.

In making the foregoing determinations, the court shall review the whole record or those parts of it cited by a party, and due account shall be taken of the rule of prejudicial error.

(e) Attorney's fees.—If the individual referred to in subsection (a) is the prevailing party in a proceeding under this subsection, attorney's fees may be allowed by the court in accordance with the standards prescribed under section 706(k) of the Civil Rights Act of 1964 (42 U.S.C. 2000e-5(k)).

SEVERABILITY—SEC. 322 [2 U.S.C. 1221]

Notwithstanding section 401 of this Act, if any provision of section 309 or 320(a)(3) is invalidated, both sections 309 and 320(a)(3) shall have no force and effect.

PAYMENTS BY THE PRESIDENT OR A MEMBER OF THE SENATE—SEC. 323 [2 U.S.C. 1222]

The President or a Member of the Senate shall reimburse the appropriate Federal account for any payment made on his or her behalf out of such account for a violation committed under the provisions of this title by the President or Member of the Senate not later than 60 days after the payment is made.

REPORTS OF SENATE COMMITTEES—SEC. 324 [2 U.S.C. 1223]

(a) Each report accompanying a bill or joint resolution of a public character reported by any committee of the Senate (except the Committee on Appropriations and the Committee on the Budget) shall contain a listing of the provisions of the bill or joint resolution that apply to Congress and an evaluation of the impact of such provisions on Congress.

(b) The provisions of this section are enacted by the Senate as an exercise of the rulemaking power of the Senate, with full recognition of the right of the Senate to change its rules, in the same manner, and to the same extent, as in the case of any other rule of the Senate.

INTERVENTION AND EXPEDITED REVIEW OF CERTAIN APPEALS—SEC. 325 [2 U.S.C. 1224]

(a) Intervention.—Because of the constitutional issues that may be raised by section 309 and section 320, any Member of the Senate may intervene as a matter of right in any proceeding under section 309 for the sole purpose of determining the constitutionality of such section.

(b) Threshold Matter.—In any proceeding under section 309 or section 320, the United States Court of Appeals for the Federal Circuit shall determine any issue presented concerning the constitutionality of such section as a threshold matter.

(c) Appeal.—

(1) In general.—An appeal may be taken directly to the Supreme Court of the United States from any interlocutory or final judgment, decree, or order issued by the United States Court of Appeals for the Federal Circuit ruling upon the constitutionality of section 309 or 320.

(2) Jurisdiction.—The Supreme Court shall, if it has not previously ruled on the question, accept jurisdiction over the appeal referred to in paragraph (1), advance the appeal on the docket and expedite the appeal to the greatest extent possible.

TITLE IV—GENERAL PROVISIONS

SEVERABILITY—SEC. 401 [42 U.S.C. 1981 note]

If any provision of this Act, or an amendment made by this Act, or the application of such provision to any person or circumstances is held to be invalid, the remainder of this Act and the amendments made by this Act, and the application of such provision to other persons and circumstances, shall not be affected.

EFFECTIVE DATE—SEC. 402 [42 U.S.C. 1981 note]

(a) In General.—Except as otherwise specifically provided, this Act and the amendments made by this Act shall take effect upon enactment.

(b) Certain Disparate Impact Cases. Notwithstanding any other provision of this Act, nothing in this Act shall apply to any disparate impact case for which a complaint was filed before March 1, 1975, and for which an initial decision was rendered after October 30, 1983.

Approved November 21, 1991.

APPENDIX 3:
EXECUTIVE ORDERS 11478 AND 13087

EXECUTIVE ORDER 11478

EQUAL EMPLOYMENT OPPORTUNITY IN THE FEDERAL GOVERNMENT

Under and by virtue of the authority vested in me as President of the United States by the Constitution and statutes of the United States, it is ordered as follows:

Section 1. It is the policy of the Government of the United States to provide equal opportunity in Federal employment for all persons, to prohibit discrimination in employment because of race, color, religion, sex, national origin, handicap, or age, and to promote the full realization of equal employment opportunity through a continuing affirmative program in each executive department and agency. This policy of equal opportunity applies to and must be an integral part of every aspect of personnel policy and practice in the employment, development, advancement, and treatment of civilian employees of the Federal Government.

Sec. 2. The head of each executive department and agency shall establish and maintain an affirmative program of equal employment opportunity for all civilian employees and applicants for employment within his jurisdiction in accordance with the policy set forth in section 1. It is the responsibility of each department and agency head, to the maximum extent possible, to provide sufficient resources to administer such a program in a positive and effective manner; assure that recruitment activities reach all sources of job candidates; utilize to the fullest extent the present skills of each employee; provide the maximum feasible opportunity to employees to enhance their skills so they may perform at their highest potential and advance in accordance with their abilities; provide training and advice to managers and supervisors to assure their understanding and implementation of the policy expressed in this Order; assure participation at the local level with other employers, schools, and public or private groups in cooperative efforts to improve community conditions which affect employability; and provide for a system within the department or agency for periodically evaluating the effectiveness with which the policy of this Order is being carried out.

Sec. 3. The Equal Employment Opportunity Commission shall be responsible for directing and furthering the implementation of the policy of the Government of the United States to provide equal opportunity in Federal employment for all employees or applicants for employment (except with regard to aliens employed outside the limits of the United States) and to prohibit discrimination in employment because of race, color, religion, sex, national origin, handicap, or age.

Sec. 4. The Equal Employment Opportunity Commission, after consultation with all affected departments and agencies, shall issue such rules, regulations, orders, and instructions and request such information from the affected departments and agencies as it deems necessary and appropriate to carry out this Order.

Sec. 5. All departments and agencies shall cooperate with and assist the Equal Employment Opportunity Commission in the performance of its functions under this Order and shall furnish the Commission such reports and information as it may request. The head of each department or agency shall comply with rules, regulations, orders and instructions issued by the Equal Employment Opportunity Commission pursuant to Section 4 of this Order.

Sec. 6. This Order applies (a) to military departments as defined in section 102 of title 5, United States Code, and executive agencies (other than the General Accounting Office) as defined in section 105 of title 5, United States Code, and to the employees thereof (including employees paid from nonappropriated funds), and (b) to those portions of the legislative and judicial branches of the Federal Government and of the Government of the District of Columbia having positions in the competitive service and to the employees in those positions. This Order does not apply to aliens employed outside the limits of the United States.

Sec. 7. Part I of Executive Order No. 11246 of September 24, 1965, and those parts of Executive Order No. 11375 of October 13, 1967, which apply to Federal employment, are hereby superseded.

Sec. 8. This Order shall be applicable to the United States Postal Service and to the Postal Rate Commission established by the Postal Reorganization Act of 1970.

EXECUTIVE ORDER 13087

FURTHER AMENDMENT TO EXECUTIVE ORDER 11478, EQUAL EMPLOYMENT OPPORTUNITY IN THE FEDERAL GOVERNMENT

By the authority vested in me as President by the Constitution and the laws of the United States, and in order to provide for a uniform policy for the Federal Government to prohibit discrimination based on sexual orientation, it is hereby ordered that Executive Order 11478, as amended, is further amended as follows:

Section 1. The first sentence of section 1 is amended by substituting "age, or sexual orientation" for "or age".

Section 2. The second sentence of section 1 is amended by striking the period and adding at the end of the sentence ", to the extent permitted by law.".

APPENDIX 4:
DIRECTORY OF UNITED STATES EQUAL EMPLOYMENT OPPORTUNITY COMMISSION OFFICES

EEOC OFFICE	ADDRESS	TELEPHONE NUMBER	TTY NUMBER
Headquarters	1801 L Street N.W., Washington, D.C. 20507	202 663-4900	202 663-4494
Albuquerque District Office	505 Marquette Street N.W., Suite 900, Albuquerque, NM 87102	505-248-5201	505-248-5240
Atlanta District Office	100 Alabama Street, Suite 4R30, Atlanta, GA 30303	404-562-6800	404-562-6801
Baltimore District Office	City Crescent Building, 3rd Floor, Baltimore, MD 21201	410-962-3932	410-962-6065
Birmingham District Office	1900 3rd Avenue North, Suite 101, Birmingham, AL 35203-2397	205-731-1359	205-731-0175
Boston Area Office	1 Congress Street, 10th Floor, Room 1001, Boston, MA 02114	617-565-3200	617-565-3204
Buffalo Local Office	6 Fountain Plaza, Suite 350, Buffalo, NY 14202	716-846-4441	716-846-5923
Charlotte District Office	129 West Trade Street, Suite 400, Charlotte, NC 28202	704-344-6682	704-344-6684

EEOC OFFICE	ADDRESS	TELEPHONE NUMBER	TTY NUMBER
Chicago District Office	500 West Madison Street, Suite 2800, Chicago, IL 60661	312-353-2713	312-353-2421
Cincinnati Area Office	525 Vine Street, Suite 810, Cincinnati, OH 45202-3122	513-684-2851	513-684-2074
Cleveland District Office	1660 West Second Street, Suite 850, Cleveland, OH 44113-1454	216-522-2001	216-522-8441
Dallas District Office	207 S. Houston Street, 3rd Floor, Dallas, TX 75202-4726	214-655-3355	214-655-3363
Denver District Office	303 E. 17th Avenue, Suite 510, Denver, CO 80203	303-866-1300	303-866-1950
Detroit District Office	477 Michigan Avenue, Room 865, Detroit, MI 48226-9704	313-226-7636	313-226-7599
El Paso Area Office	The Commons, Building C, Suite 100, 4171 N. Mesa Street, El Paso, TX 79902	915-534-6550	915-534-6545
Fresno Local Office	1265 West Shaw Avenue, Suite 103, Fresno, CA 93711	209-487-5793	209-487-5837
Greensboro Local Office	801 Summit Avenue, Greensboro, NC 27405-7813	910-333-5174	910-333-5542
Greenville Local Office	Wachovia Building, Suite 530, 15 South Main Street, Greenville, SC 29601	803-241-4400	803-241-4403

EEOC OFFICE	ADDRESS	TELEPHONE NUMBER	TTY NUMBER
Honolulu Local Office	300 Ala Moana Boulevard, Room 7123-A, P.O. Box 50082, Honolulu, HI 96850-0051	808-541-3120	808-541-3131
Houston District Office	1919 Smith Street, 7th Floor, Houston, TX 77002	713-209-3320	713-209-3367
Indianapolis District Office	101 W. Ohio Street, Suite 1900, Indiana, IN 46204-4203	317-226-7212	317-226-5162
Jackson Area Office	207 West Amite Street, Jackson, MS 39201	601-965-4537	601-965-4915
Kansas City Area Office	400 State Avenue, Suite 905, Kansas City, KS 66101	913-551-5655	913-551-5657
Little Rock Area Office	425 West Capitol Avenue, Suite 625, Little Rock, AR 72201	501-324-5060	501-324-5481
Los Angeles District Office	255 E. Temple, 4th Floor, Los Angeles, CA 90012	213-894-1000	213-894-1121
Louisville Area Office	600 Dr. Martin Luther King Jr. Place, Suite 268, Louisville, KY 40202	502-582-6082	502-582-6285
Memphis District Office	1407 Union Avenue, Suite 521, Memphis, TN 38104	901-544-0115	901-544-0112
Miami District Office	One Biscayne Tower, 2 South Biscayne Boulevard, Suite 2700, Miami, FL 33131	305-536-4491	305-536-5721
Milwaukee District Office	310 West Wisconsin Avenue, Suite 800, Milwaukee, WI 53203-2292	414-297-1111	414-297-1115

EEOC OFFICE	ADDRESS	TELEPHONE NUMBER	TTY NUMBER
Minneapolis Area Office	330 South Second Avenue, Suite 430, Minneapolis, MN 55401-2224	612-335-4040	612-335-4045
Nashville Area Office	50 Vantage Way, Suite 202, Nashville, TN 37228	615-736-5820	615-736-5870
Newark Area Office	1 Newark Center, 21st Floor, Newark, NJ 07102-5233	201-645-6383	201-645-3004
New Orleans District Office	701 Loyola Avenue, Suite 600, New Orleans, LA 70113-9936	504-589-2329	504-589-2958
New York District Office	201 Varick Street, Room 1009, New York, NY 10014	212-741-8815	212-741-2783
Norfolk Area Office	World Trade Center, 101 West Main Street, Suite 4300, Norfolk, VA 23510	804-441-3470	804-441-3578
Oakland Local Office	1301 Clay Street, Suite 1170-N, Oakland, CA 94612-5217	510-637-3230	510-637-3234
Oklahoma Area Office	210 Park Avenue, Oklahoma City, OK 73102	405-231-4911	405-231-5745
Philadelphia District Office	21 South 5th Street, 4th Floor, Philadelphia, PA 19106	215-451-5800	215-451-5814
Phoenix District Office	3300 N. Central Avenue, Phoenix, AZ 85012-1848	602-640-5000	602-640-5072
Pittsburgh Area Office	1001 Liberty Avenue, Suite 300, Pittsburgh, PA 15222-4187	412-644-3444	412-644-2720

EEOC OFFICE	ADDRESS	TELEPHONE NUMBER	TTY NUMBER
Raleigh Area Office	1309 Annapolis Drive, Raleigh, NC 27608-2129	919-856-4064	919-856-4296
Richmond Area Office	3600 West Broad Street, Room 229, Richmond, VA 23230	804-278-4651	804-278-4654
San Antonio District Office	5410 Fredericksburg Road, Suite 200, San Antonio, TX 78229-3555	210-229-4810	210-229-4858
San Diego Area Office	401 B Street, Suite 1550, San Diego, CA 92101	619-557-7235	619-557-7232
San Francisco District Office	901 Market Street, Suite 500, San Francisco, CA 94103	415-356-5100	415-356-5098
San Jose Local Office	96 North 3rd Street, Suite 200, San Jose, CA 95112	408-291-7352	408-291-7374
San Juan Area Office	525 F.D. Roosevelt Avenue, Plaza Las Americas, Suite 1202, San Juan, Puerto Rico 00918-8001	787-771-1464	787-771-1484
Savannah Local Office	410 Mall Boulevard, Suite G, Savannah, GA 31406-4821	912-652-4234	912-652-4439
Seattle District Office	Federal Office Building, 909 First Avenue, Suite 400, Seattle, WA 98104-1061	206-220-6883	206-220-6882
St. Louis District Office	Robert A. Young Building, 1222 Spruce Street, Room 8.100, St. Louis, MO 63103	314-539-7800	314-539-7803

EEOC OFFICE	ADDRESS	TELEPHONE NUMBER	TTY NUMBER
Tampa Area Office	501 East Polk Street, 10th Floor, Tampa, FL 33602	813-228-2310	813-228-2003
Washington Field Office	1400 L Street N.W., Suite 200, Washington, D.C. 20005	Phone: 202-275-7377	202-275-7518

Source: U.S. Equal Employment Opportunity Commission.

APPENDIX 5:
DIRECTORY OF UNITED STATES EQUAL EMPLOYMENT OPPORTUNITY COMMISSION MEDIATION OFFICES

EEOC MEDIATION OFFICE	ADDRESS	TELEPHONE NUMBER	TTY NUMBER	FAX NUMBER
Albuquerque	505 Marquette NW, Suite 900, Albuquerque, New Mexico 87102	(505) 248-5193	(505) 248-5240	(505) 248-5196
Atlanta	100 Alabama Street SW, Suite 4R30, Atlanta, Georgia 30303	(404) 562-6841	(404 562-6801	(404) 562-6974
Baltimore	City Crescent Building, 10 South Howard Street, 3rd Floor, Baltimore, Maryland 21201	(410) 962-6606	(410) 962-6065	(410) 962-3706
Birmingham	1900 3rd Avenue North, Suite 101, Birmingham, Alabama 35203-2397	(205) 731-0810	(205) 731-0175	(205) 731-1002
Charlotte	129 West Trade Street, Suite 400, Charlotte, North Carolina 28202	(704) 344-6689	(704) 344-6684	(704) 3446750

EEOC MEDIATION OFFICE	ADDRESS	TELEPHONE NUMBER	TTY NUMBER	FAX NUMBER
Chicago	500 West Madison Street, Suite 2800, Chicago, Illinois 60661	(312) 353-1099	(312) 353-2421	(312) 353-6676
Cleveland	1660 West Second Street, Suite 850, Cleveland, Ohio 44113-1454	(216) 522-7678	(216) 522-8441	(216) 522-7389
Dallas	207 S. Houston Street, 3rd Floor, Dallas, Texas 75202-4726	(214) 655-3348	(214) 665-3363	(214) 665-3443
Denver	303 E. 17th Avenue, Suite 510, Denver, Colorado 80203	(303) 866-1313	(303) 866-1950	(303) 866-1085
Detroit	477 Michigan Avenue, Room 865, Detroit, Michigan 48226-2523	(313) 226-4666	(313) 226-7599	(313) 226-3045
Houston	Mickey Leland Federal Building, 1919 Smith Street, 7th Floor, Houston, Texas 77002-8049	(713) 209-3433	(713) 209-3439	(713) 209-3317
Indianapolis	101 West Ohio Street, Suite 1900, Indianapolis, Indiana 46204-4203	(317) 226-6422	(317) 226-5162	(317) 226-5471
Los Angeles	255 E. Temple Street, 4th Floor, Los Angeles, California 90012	(213) 894-1030	(213) 894-1121	(213) 894-8385

EEOC MEDIATION OFFICE	ADDRESS	TELEPHONE NUMBER	TTY NUMBER	FAX NUMBER
Memphis	1407 Union Avenue, Suite 621, Memphis, Tennessee 38104	(901) 544-0131	(901) 544-0112	(901) 544-0126
Miami	One Biscayne Tower, 2 South Biscayne Boulevard, Suite 2700, Miami, Florida 33131	(305) 530-6002	(305) 536-5721	(305) 536-4494
Milwaukee	310 West Wisconsin Avenue, Suite 800, Milwaukee, Wisconsin 53203-2292	(414) 297-1276	(414) 297-1115	(414) 297-3125
New Orleans	701 Loyola Avenue, Suite 600, New Orleans, Louisiana 70113-9936	(504) 589-6819	(504) 589-2958	(504) 589-3626
New York	201 Varick Street, Room 1009, New York, New York 10014	(212) 620-0443	(212) 741-2783	(212) 741-3080 (212) 620-0070
Philadelphia	21 South 5th Street, Suite 400, Philadelphia, Pennsylvania 19106-2515	(215) 440-2819	(215) 440-2610	(215) 440-2822
Phoenix	3300 N. Central Avenue, Suite 690, Phoenix, Arizona 85012-2504	(602) 640-5022	(602) 640-5072	(602) 640-5071

EEOC MEDIATION OFFICE	ADDRESS	TELEPHONE NUMBER	TTY NUMBER	FAX NUMBER
San Antonio	5410 Fredericksburg Road, Suite 200, San Antonio, Texas 78229-3555	(210) 281-2507	(210) 281-7610	(210) 281-2512
San Francisco	901 Market Street, Suite 500, San Francisco, California 94103	(415) 356-5044	(415) 356-5098	(415) 356-5116
Seattle	Federal Office Building, 909 First Avenue, Suite 400, Seattle, Washington 98104-1061	(206) 220-6860	(206) 220-6882	(206) 220-6911
St. Louis	Robert A. Young Building, 1222 Spruce Street, Room 8.100, St. Louis, Missouri 63103	(314) 539-7831	not listed	(913) 551-5806
Washington Field Office	1400 L Street NW, Suite 200, Washington, D.C. 20005	(202) 275-0068	(202) 275-7518	(202) 632-0076

APPENDIX 6:
DIRECTORY OF STATE AND LOCAL EQUAL EMPLOYMENT AND CIVIL RIGHTS OFFICES

STATE	AGENCY	ADDRESS	TELEPHONE NUMBER	FAX NUMBER	TDD NUMBER
Alabama	Civil Rights/Equal Employment Office	Department of Human Resources, 50 Ripley Street, Montgomery, AL 36130	(334) 242-1550	(334) 353-1491	(334) 242-0196
Alaska	Alaska State Commission for Human Rights	800 A Street, Suite 204, Anchorage, AK 99501-3669	(907) 274-4692	none listed	(907) 276-3177

STATE	AGENCY	ADDRESS	TELEPHONE NUMBER	FAX NUMBER	TDD NUMBER
Arizona	Arizona Civil Rights Division	Office of the Arizona Attorney General, 1275 W. Washington Street, Phoenix, AZ 85007-2926	(602) 542-5263	(602) 542-1275	(602) 542-5002
California	California Fair Employment & Housing Commission	2014 T Street, Ste 210, Sacramento, CA 95814-6835	(800) 884-1684	none listed	none listed
Colorado	Colorado Civil Rights Division	1560 Broadway, Room 1050, Denver, CO 80202-5143	(303) 894-2997	(303) 894-7830	(303) 894-7832
Connecticut	Connecticut Commission on Human Rights and Opportunity	21 Grand Street, Hartford, CT 06106	(860) 541-3400	(860) 246-5068	(860) 541-3459
Delaware	Delaware Division of Human Relations	820 N. French Street, 4th Floor, Wilmington, DE 19801	(302) 577-5050	(302) 577-3486	none listed

STATE	AGENCY	ADDRESS	TELEPHONE NUMBER	FAX NUMBER	TDD NUMBER
District of Columbia	Department of Human Rights	One Judiciary Square, 441 4th Street NW, Suite 970 N, Washington, DC 20001	(202) 724-3900	(202) 724-8786	none listed
Florida	Florida Commission on Human Relations	325 John Knox Road, Bldg. F, Suite 240, Tallahassee, FL 32303-4149	(850) 488-7082	(850) 488-5291	(800) 342-8170
Georgia	Georgia Commission on Equal Opportunity	710 International Tower, 229 Peachtree Street NE, Atlanta, GA 30303-1605	(404) 656-1736	(404) 656-4399	none listed
Hawaii	Hawaii Civil Rights Commission	830 Punchbowl Street, Room 411, Honolulu, HI 96813	(808) 586-8636	(808) 586-8655	none listed
Idaho	Idaho Human Rights Commission	1109 Main Street, Suite 400, Boise, ID 83720-0040	(208) 334-2873	(208) 334-2664	(208) 334-4751
Illinois	Illinois Department of Human Rights	100 W. Randolph Street, Suite 10-100, Chicago, IL 60601	(312) 814-6200	(312) 814-6251	(312) 263-1579

STATE	AGENCY	ADDRESS	TELEPHONE NUMBER	FAX NUMBER	TDD NUMBER
Indiana	Indiana Civil Rights Commission	100 N. Senate Avenue, Room N103, Indianapolis, IN 46204	(317) 232-2600	(317) 232-6580	(800) 743-3333
Iowa	Iowa Civil Rights Commission (ICRC)	211 E. Maple Street, 2nd Floor, Des Moines, IA 50319	(515) 281-4121	(515) 242-5840	none listed
Kansas	Kansas Human Rights Commission	900 SW Jackson, Suite 851-S, Topeka, KS 66612-1258	(785) 296-3206	(785)296-0589	(785) 296-0245
Kentucky	Kentucky Commission on Human Rights	332 W. Broadway, Suite 700, Louisville, KY 40202	(502) 595-4024	(502) 595-4801	(502) 595-4084
Louisiana	Louisiana Commission on Human Rights	1001 N. 23rd St., Suite 262, Baton Rouge, LA 70802	(225) 342-6969	(225) 342-2063	(888) 248-0859
Maine	Maine Human Rights Commission	51 State House Station, Augusta, ME 04333-0051	(207) 624-6050	(207) 624-6063	(207) 624-6064

STATE	AGENCY	ADDRESS	TELEPHONE NUMBER	FAX NUMBER	TDD NUMBER
Maryland	Maryland Commission on Human Relations	6 St. Paul Street, 9th Floor, Suite 900, Baltimore, MD 21202-2274	(410) 767-8600	(410) 333-1841	(410) 333-1737
Massachusetts	Massachusetts Commission Against Discrimination	One Ashburton Place, Room 601, Boston, MA 02108	(617) 727-3990	(617) 720-6053	(617) 720-6054
Michigan	Michigan Department of Civil Rights	State of Michigan Plaza Bldg., 6th Flr., 1200 Sixth Ave., Detroit, MI 48226	(313) 256-2663	(313) 256-2167	none listed
Minnesota	Minnesota Department of Human Rights	Army Corps of Engineers Center, 190 E. 5th Street, St. Paul, MN 55101	(651) 296-5663	(651) 296-1283	none listed
Missouri	Missouri Commission on Human Rights	3315 West Truman Boulevard, Jefferson City, MO 65102-1129	(573) 751-3325	(573) 751-2905	(573) 526-5091

STATE	AGENCY	ADDRESS	TELEPHONE NUMBER	FAX NUMBER	TDD NUMBER
Montana	Montana Human Rights Bureau	1625 11th Avenue, P.O. Box 1728, Helena, MT 59624-1728	(406) 444-2884	none listed	none listed
Nebraska	Nebraska Equal Opportunity Commission (NEOC)	Nebraska State Office Building, 301 Centennial Mall South, 5th Floor, Lincoln, NE 68509-4934	(402) 471-2024	(402) 471-4059	none listed
Nevada	Nevada Equal Rights Commission	1515 E. Tropicana Avenue, Ste. 500, Las Vegas, NV 89119-6522	(702) 486-7161	(702) 486-7054	none listed
New Hampshire	New Hampshire Commission for Human Rights	2 Chenelle Drive, Concord, NH 03301-8501	(603) 271-2767	(603) 271-6339	none listed
New Jersey	New Jersey Department of Law and Safety Division of Civil Rights	31 Clinton Street, Newark, NJ 07102	(201) 648-2700	(201) 648-4405	none listed

STATE	AGENCY	ADDRESS	TELEPHONE NUMBER	FAX NUMBER	TDD NUMBER
New Mexico	New Mexico Department of Labor Human Rights Division	1596 Pacheco Street, Suite 103, Santa Fe, NM 87505	(505) 827-6838	(505) 827-6878	none listed
New York	New York State Attorney General Civil Rights Bureau	120 Broadway, 23rd Floor, New York, NY 10271	(212) 416-8250	(212) 416-8074	none listed
North Carolina	North Carolina Human Relations Commission	217 W. Jones Street, 4th Floor, Raleigh, NC 27603	(919) 733-7996	none listed	none listed
North Dakota	North Dakota Department of Labor	none listed	(701) 328-2660	none listed	none listed
Ohio	Ohio Civil Rights Commission	1111 E. Broad Street, Suite 301, Columbus, OH 43205-1379	(614) 466-5928	(614) 466-6250	(614) 752-2391
Oklahoma	Oklahoma Human Rights Commission	2101 N. Lincoln Boulevard, Room 480, Oklahoma City, OK 73105	(405) 521-2360	(405) 522-3635	(405) 522-3993

STATE	AGENCY	ADDRESS	TELEPHONE NUMBER	FAX NUMBER	TDD NUMBER
Oregon	Oregon Civil Rights Division	800 N.E. Oregon, Suite 1070, Portland, OR 97232	(503) 731-4200	none listed	(503) 731-4106
Pennsylvania	Pennsylvania Attorney General	Civil Rights Enforcement Section, 14th Floor, Strawberry Square, Harrisburg, PA 17120	(717) 787-0822	(717) 787-1190	none listed
Rhode Island	Rhode Island Commission for Human Rights	10 Abbott Park Place, Providence, RI 02903-3768	(401) 277-2661	(401) 277-2616	(401) 222-2664
South Carolina	South Carolina Human Affairs Commission	2611 Forest Drive, Suite 200 , P.O Box 4490 Columbia, SC 29240	(803) 737-7800	(803) 253-4125	none listed
South Dakota	South Dakota Division of Human Rights	18 W. Capitol Avenue, Pierre, SD 57501	(605) 773-4493	(605) 773-6893	none listed
Tennessee	Tennessee Human Rights Commission	530 Church Street, Suite 400, Nashville, TN 37243-0745	(615) 741-5825	(615) 532-2197	none listed

STATE	AGENCY	ADDRESS	TELEPHONE NUMBER	FAX NUMBER	TDD NUMBER
Texas	Texas Commission on Human Rights	P.O. Box 13006, Austin, Texas 78711-3006	(512) 437-3450	(512) 437-3478	(512) 371-7473
Utah	Utah Anti-Discrimination Division	160 East 300 South, 3rd Floor, Salt Lake City, UT 84111	(801) 530-6801	(801) 530-7609	(801) 530-7685
Vermont	State of Vermont Attorney General	Civil Rights Unit, 109 State Street, Montpelier, VT 05609	(802) 828-5511	(802) 828-3187	(802) 828-3665
Virginia	Virginia Council on Human Rights	Washington Building, Suite 1202, 1100 Bank Street, Richmond, VA 23219	(804) 225-2292	none listed	none listed
Washington	Washington State Human Rights Commission	711 S. Capitol Way, # 402, Olympia, WA 98504-2490	(360) 753-6770	(360) 586-2282	(800) 300-7525
West Virginia	West Virginia Human Rights Commission	1321 Plaza East, Room 108A, Charleston, WV 25301-1400	(304) 558-2616	(304) 558-0085	(304) 558-2976

STATE	AGENCY	ADDRESS	TELEPHONE NUMBER	FAX NUMBER	TDD NUMBER
Wisconsin	Wisconsin Equal Rights Division, Civil Rights Bureau,	1 South Pinckney Street, Room 320, Madison, WI 53708	(608) 266-6860	(608) 267-4592	
Wyoming	Wyoming Department of Employment/Fair Employment Programs	6101 Yellowstone, Room 259C, Cheyenne, WY 82002	(307) 777-7261	(307) 777-5633	none listed

APPENDIX 7:
DIRECTORY OF REGIONAL OFFICES OF THE UNITED STATES DEPARTMENT OF LABOR—WOMEN'S BUREAU

REGION	ADDRESS	TELEPHONE NUMBER	AREAS COVERED
Headquarters	U.S. Department of Labor, Washington, D.C. 20210	(800) 827-5335	All Regional Offices
Region I: Boston	J.F. Kennedy Building, Government Center, Room E-270, Boston, MA 02203	(617) 565-1988	Connecticut, Maine, Massachusetts, New Hampshire, Rhode Island, Vermont
Region II: New York	201 Varick Street, Room 601, New York, NY 10014	(212) 337-2389	New Jersey, New York, Puerto Rico, U.S. Virgin Islands
Region III: Philadelphia	Gateway Building, 3535 Market Street, Room 2450, Philadelphia, PA 19104	(215) 596-1183	Delaware, District of Columbia, Maryland, Pennsylvania, Virginia, West Virginia
Region IV: Atlanta	Atlanta Federal Center, 61 Forsyth Street SW, Suite 7T95, Atlanta, GA 30367	(404) 562-2336	Alabama, Florida, Georgia, Kentucky, Mississippi, North Carolina, South Carolina, Tennessee
Region V: Chicago	230 S. Dearborn Street, Room 1022, Chicago, IL 60604	(312) 353-6985	Illinois, Indiana, Michigan, Minnesota, Ohio, Wisconsin

REGION	ADDRESS	TELEPHONE NUMBER	AREAS COVERED
Region VI: Dallas	Federal Building, 525 Griffin Street, Dallas, TX 75202	(214) 767-6985	Arkansas, Louisiana, New Mexico, Oklahoma, Texas
Region VII: Kansas City	City Center Square Building, 1100 Main Street, Suite 1230, Kansas City, MO 64105	(816) 426-6108	Iowa, Kansas, Missouri, Nebraska
Region VIII: Denver	1801 California Street, Suite 905, Denver, CO 80202-2614	(303) 844-1286	Colorado, Montana, North Dakota, South Dakota, Utah, Wyoming
Region IX: San Francisco	71 Stevenson Street, Suite 927, San Francisco, CA 94105	(415) 975-4750	Arizona, California, Guam, Hawaii, Nevada
Region X: Seattle	1111 Third Avenue, Room 885, Seattle, WA 98101-3211	(206) 553-1534	Alaska, Idaho, Oregon, Washington

APPENDIX 8:
DESIGNATION OF LEGAL
REPRESENTATIVE

TO: U.S. OFFICE OF SPECIAL COUNSEL
1730 M Street, N.W., Suite 201
Washington, D.C. 20036-4505

RE: Designation of Personal Legal Representative
OSC Case No. _____

By signing below you indicate that you have voluntarily chosen the designated individual to serve as your personal legal counsel for the purpose of providing advice and counsel in connection with the Office of Special Counsel case identified below. The representative designated by you must also indicate agreement to such designation by signing below.

I hereby designate _____ to serve as my personal legal representative during the course of this investigation.

_____

Name/Address of Witness/Subject

_____

Signature of Witness/Subject _____ Date_____

Name/Address of Personal Legal Representative

_____

Signature of Representative _____ Date_____

Telephone Number of Representative: _____

APPENDIX 9:
SAMPLE WORKPLACE HARASSMENT POLICY FOR A MUNICIPALITY

WORKPLACE HARASSMENT POLICY

I. PURPOSE

The purpose of this policy is to define the City's policy and procedures regarding the prohibition of harassment and discrimination and give notice to all employees. As part of the City's continuing efforts to ensure full equal employment opportunity and conform with Title VII of the Civil Rights Act of 1964, the guidelines issued by the Equal Employment Opportunity Commission, and the regulations issued by the State Fair Employment and Housing Commission, this policy shall be distributed to all current and future employees. Utilizing this policy and procedure does not waive an employee's rights to pursue action with the agencies mentioned above or to initiate civil action. It is not the intent of this policy to regulate the social interaction of relationships freely entered into by or between City employees.

II. POLICY

The City is committed to creating and maintaining a work environment that is free of all forms of harassment or intimidation, including sexual harassment. Sexual harassment is a form of sex discrimination, is an abuse of power, and is an unlawful employment practice prohibited by State and Federal Law. It debilitates morale and interferes with work productivity. It is the policy of the City that harassment and discrimination are unacceptable and will not be condoned or tolerated on the part of any employee. The City shall take preventative, corrective, and disciplinary action for behavior that violates this policy or the rights and privileges it is designed to protect. In addition, individual employees can be held personally liable for acts of sexual harassment.

An employee who believes he/she has been harassed either in the process of applying for a position, carrying out the duties of the job, outside the work place by another employee, or by someone such as citizens, contractors, or consultants doing business with the City are encouraged to use the complaint process and procedures that are outlined in this policy. An employee who files a complaint of harassment shall be free from reprisals or retaliation, regardless of the outcome. Retaliation in any form is considered a serious violation of this policy. Anyone engaging in subtle or overt forms of retaliation shall be subject to an investigation and appropriate disciplinary action.

III. DEFINITIONS AND EXAMPLES

A. Harassment of a Sexual Nature

Sexual harassment has been specifically defined by the Equal Employment Opportunity Commission as follows:

> Unwelcome sexual advances, requests for sexual favors, or other verbal, visual, or physical conduct of a sexual nature constitutes sexual harassment when:
>
> 1. Submission to such conduct is made either explicitly or implicitly a term or condition of an employee's employment; or
>
> 2. Submission to, or rejection of, such conduct by an employee is used as the basis for employment decisions affecting the employee; or
>
> 3. Such conduct has the purpose or effect of unreasonably interfering with an individual's work performance or creates on intimidating, hostile, or offensive working environment.

Sexual harassment refers to behavior which is not welcomed, is personally offensive to the victim, and interferes with the ability to effectively carry out the duties of his/her position or co-workers' positions. Differences in individual values and culturally diverse customs may make it difficult for employees to recognize their own behavior or that of their peers, subordinates, or non-employees as sexual harassment. An investigation and decision based on all the available facts must be made to determine whether a particular action or incident constitutes sexual harassment. Negative consequences to the offender places a responsibility on supervisors and employees to report factual and truthful information in filing and investigating complaints of sexual harassment.

B. Examples of Harassment

Harassment may take many forms, including but not limited to:

1. Verbal Harassment—For example, epithets, derogatory comments or slurs on the basis of race, religious creed, color, national origin, ancestry, physical handicap, medical condition, age, marital status, sex, sexual orientation, political opinions or affiliations, or lawful employee organization activities. Verbal harassment may also include sexual remarks or well-intentioned compliments about a person's clothing, body, or sexual activities.

2. Physical Harassment—For example, assault, unwelcome touching, impeding or blocking movement, and/or any physical interference with normal work or movement when directed at an individual on the basis of race, religious creed, color, national origin, ancestry, physical handicap, medical condition, age, marital status, sex, sexual orientation, political opinions or affiliations, or lawful employee organization activities.

3. Visual Forms of Harassment—For example, derogatory posters, notices, bulletins, cartoons, drawings, or other advertisements on the basis of race, religious creed, color, national origin, ancestry, physical handicap, medical condition, age, marital status, sex, sexual orientation, political opinions or affiliations, or lawful employee organization activities. This includes, but is not limited to, posters, magazines, videos, Internet sites, or other electronic media of a sexual nature.

4. Sexual Favors—Unwelcome sexual advances, requests for sexual favors, and other verbal or physical conduct of a sexual nature which are implicitly or explicitly a term or condition of an employee's employment, are used as the basis of employment decisions, or affect or interfere with the employee's work performance.

5. Hostile Environment—Conduct including the above-referenced behaviors that has the purpose or effect of creating an intimidating, hostile, or offensive work environment.

IV. RESPONSIBILITIES

1. The City Manager shall be responsible for assigning responsibility and accountability for implementation of the City's harassment and discrimination policy and procedures. He/She shall take all steps necessary to set a positive example and to support and encourage actions and attitudes in the organization that prevent harassment and discrimination from occurring. He/She shall direct the investigation and re-

spond to all complaints involving Department Heads and the Assistant City Manager.

2. The Human Resources Director shall be responsible for ensuring that all complaints of harassment and discrimination are investigated thoroughly and are responded to in a timely fashion and arrange for periodic training for all employees, including supervisors and managers. Formal training shall be on a semi-annual basis at a minimum and employees shall sign signature sheets as evidence of training. He/She shall assist, advise, or consult with employees, supervisors, and managers regarding the harassment and discrimination policy, complaint procedures, and incidents. He/She shall maintain current knowledge of harassment and discrimination legal issues.

3. Department Heads, Division Managers, and Supervisors shall be responsible for informing employees of the City's policy on harassment and discrimination. They shall take all steps necessary to set a positive example and to prevent harassment and discrimination from occurring. Managers and supervisors are responsible for acts of harassment and discrimination in the work place by employees and non-employees and become legally liable when the manager/supervisor knows, or should have known, of the conduct but fails to take immediate and appropriate corrective action. Managers and supervisors shall assist, advise, or consult with employees and the Human Resources Director regarding harassment and discrimination policy, complaint procedures, and incidents. Managers and supervisors shall assist in the investigation of complaints involving employee(s) in their departments; and if the complaint is substantiated, shall recommend appropriate corrective or disciplinary action in accordance with City/District Personnel Rules, up to and including discharge. Managers and supervisors shall participate in periodic training and shall schedule employees for training.

4. All Employees shall treat each other with respect and consideration and shall not engage in actions or behaviors that violate or encourage violation of the City's harassment and discrimination policy. Employees shall participate in periodic training and shall fully cooperate with investigation of harassment and discrimination incident(s). Employees who believe they have been the subject of harassment or discrimination are strongly encouraged to seek assistance, consultation and support, and/or to utilize the procedures in this policy to assure that the problem is identified, investigated, and resolved as expediently as possible.

V. COMPLAINT PROCESS AND PROCEDURES—SEXUAL HARASSMENT COMPLAINTS

To accommodate the unique and sensitive nature of sexual harassment complaints, a separate process is provided for the primary purpose of resolving these complaints at the earliest possible date. These procedures are contained in this document. Employees shall make a decision to utilize this process or another (e.g. grievance) but not both. To address other kinds of discrimination or harassment, employees should utilize existing grievance procedures in the Personnel Rules or applicable Memoranda of Understanding.

During the informal and/or formal complaint process outlined below, every effort shall be made to protect the privacy of the individuals involved in the complaint, as long as this does not compromise safety or a prompt and thorough investigation. Verbal information and written documents shall be restricted to individuals responsible for receiving, investigating and responding to the complaint. Complaints involving alleged criminal behavior shall be referred to the appropriate law enforcement agency. The Department Head shall be apprised of all complaints, unless he/she is a named party in the complaint. All employees involved in a harassment complaint may be represented by a person of their choosing (at their own expense) during the informal and/or formal complaint process.

Complaint Procedure

1. Protest or Object to the Harassment

An employee who believes he/she is a victim of harassment or discrimination may prefer to address the issue directly with the individual(s) involved. Many victims find using this informal approach to be effective. Firmly telling the other offender to stop may improve the situation. However, anyone uncomfortable with this approach or unable to alleviate the problem with this method is encouraged to proceed to the next step.

Using the informal complaint procedure is not comfortable for everyone or appropriate for every situation. Protesting or objecting to the conduct with the individual(s) involved is not a prerequisite to filling a formal or an informal complaint.

2. Seek Assistance, Advice or Consultation

Obtain the assistance of, advice from, or consultation with a supervisor, manager, Department Head, Human Resources Director, or Employee Assistance Program representative. Sexual harassment problems brought to the attention of supervisory or management representatives of the City through the informal complaint procedure shall be taken seriously and addressed promptly. Management and supervisory personnel shall advise the Human Resources Director of all informal complaints brought to their attention.

Due to the nature and seriousness of sexual harassment, all incidences and complaints shall be investigated. Investigations will remain confidential to the extent possible and be conducted in a thorough and sensitive manner.

3. File a Written Complaint

If previously outlined efforts do not resolve the problem to the victim's satisfaction or within a reasonable time frame, the employee shall proceed with the formal complaint process. An employee who believes he or she has been the subject of sexual harassment or discrimination and either has not resolved the problem or does not feel comfortable utilizing the informal complaint process, shall report the incident(s) to the Department Head and the Human Resources Director in writing. Employees are encouraged to use the Confidential Complaint Form for this purpose.

4. Receiving and Investigating Complaints

The Human Resources Director and Department Head (unless either party is named in the complaint) shall coordinate the actions of all individuals involved in the receipt, investigation, and resolution of formal complaints. Department Heads may be in a position to receive a complaint and will consult with Human Resources as soon as possible thereafter. He/She may utilize the services of attorneys, consultants, investigators, or other specialists as appropriate.

The investigation shall include, but is not limited to, the following:

(a) a review of all available information regarding the alleged conduct, giving consideration to the records, the totality of circumstances, the nature of the conduct or actions, and the context in which the alleged incident occurred;

(b) the identification and interview of the accused, witnesses, and supervisors, retrieval and review of documents or evidence including, but not limited to, computer records, work schedules, letters, telephone messages, personnel files, gifts, or cards.

(c) preparation of a written report by the investigating party submitted to the City Manager and Human Resources Director that includes allegations of the alleged victim, the accused's response, persons interviewed and their credibility, findings of facts and supporting evidence, conclusions about the allegations, and recommendations for corrective actions or discipline in accordance with City/District Personnel Rules; and

(d) completion of the investigation and response to the complaint within thirty (30) days (whenever possible) by the Human Resources Director. Both the complainant and the accused shall be notified of the outcome of the investigation and the response to the complaint.

Resolution of a Complaint

1. If the complaint is substantiated, through informal or formal procedures, this policy shall be reviewed with the accused and appropriate corrective or disciplinary action shall be recommended by the employee's Department Head, up to and including termination in accordance with City/District Personnel Rules. Employees disciplined for substantial complaints of harassment or discrimination may appeal the Department Head's decision in accordance with Personnel Rule 14.

2. If the complaint is not substantiated, the Human Resources Director shall conduct a review and assessment with the complainant and the accused individually. The review and assessment shall address issues of sensitivity, confidentiality, and the seriousness of sexual harassment allegations.

VI. POLICY IMPLEMENTATION

Each Department Head is responsible for ensuring that the workplace is free of harassment and discrimination by implementing and documenting the following measures:

1. Setting a positive example of behavior appropriate to the workplace and encouraging all department personnel to do likewise;

2. Posting copies of the policy and this procedure in conspicuous places;

3. Having managers and supervisors inform their employees of the City policy and complaint resolution procedures;

4. Encouraging employees to report instances of harassment or discrimination to the appropriate party promptly;

5. Holding employees, supervisors and managers accountable for following the provisions of this workplace harassment policy and procedures; and

6. Requiring managers, supervisors and employees to attend training or read materials supplied by the City to increase awareness of and sensitivity to the problem of harassment and discrimination.

The City's policy shall be distributed to all employees, accompanied by training on the subject. New employees shall receive a copy of the policy with orientations. New supervisors or Department Heads will be advised of the responsibilities of their position with regard to harassment and discrimination prevention and reporting, and investigation procedures.

Suggestions for improvements to the policy can be communicated to the Human Resources Director at any time. The policy will be reviewed periodically and revised as needed to comply with laws and legal recommendations. Confidential surveys may be conducted to determine if harassment has or is occurring in the workplace that has not been reported.

VII. EFFECTIVE DATE

Passed and adopted by resolutions of the City Council on _____.

APPENDIX 10:
DIRECTORY OF UNITED STATES EQUAL EMPLOYMENT OPPORTUNITY SMALL BUSINESS LIAISONS

EEOC LIAISON OFFICE	CONTACT	TELEPHONE NUMBER	E-MAIL
Albuquerque	Albert Sanchez	(505) 248-5210	Albert.sanchez@eeoc.gov
Atlanta	William Rantin	(404) 562-6826	William.rantin@eeoc.gov
Baltimore	Erica Cryor	(410) 962-4194	Erica.cryor@eeoc.gov
Birmingham	Beverly Hinton	(205) 731-0969	Beverly.hinton@eeoc.gov
Charlotte	Billy Sanders	(704) 344-6735	Billy.sanders@eeoc.gov
Chicago	Rita Coffey	(312) 353-7254	Rita.coffey@eeoc.gov
Cincinnati	Wilma Javey	(513) 684-2379	wilma.javey@eeoc.gov
Cleveland	Cynthia Stankiewicz	(216) 522-7679	cynthia.stankiewicz@eeoc.gov
Dallas	Edward Elizondo	(214) 655-3386	Edward.elizondo@eeoc.gov
Denver	Patricia McMahon	(303) 866-1344	patricia.mcmahon@eeoc.gov
Detroit	Jesse Vidaurri	(313) 226-7635	jesse.vidaurri@eeoc.gov
El Paso	Jose Gurany	(915) 534-6688	Jose.gurany@eeoc.gov

EEOC LIAISON OFFICE	CONTACT	TELEPHONE NUMBER	E-MAIL
Fresno	David Rodriguez	(559) 487-5793	David.rodriguez@eeoc.gov
Greensboro	Glenn Todd	(336) 547-4080	glenn.todd@eeoc.gov
Greenville	Patricia Fuller	(864) 241-4410	Patricia.fuller@eeoc.gov
Honolulu	Timothy Riera	(808) 541-3722	timothy.riera@eeoc.gov
Houston	Joe Bontke	(713) 209-3436	joe.bontke@eeoc.gov
Indianapolis	Joy Pentz	(317) 226-5372	joy.pentz@eeoc.gov
Jackson	Linda Walker	(901) 965-5635	linda.walker@eeoc.gov
Kansas City	Billie Ashton	(913) 551-5842	billie.ashton@eeoc.gov
Little Rock	Karen Klugh	(501) 324-6372	karen.klugh@eeoc.gov
Los Angeles	Santos Albarran	(213) 894-1045	Santos.albarran@eeoc.gov
Memphis	Lola Bufford	(901) 544-0082	lola.bufford@eeoc.gov
Miami	Nitza Wright	(305) 530-6024	nitza.wright@eeoc.gov
Milwaukee	Maria Flores	(414) 297-3594	maria.flores@eeoc.gov
Nashville	Sarah Smith	(615) 736-5824	sarah.smith@eeoc.gov
New Orleans	Tydell Nealy	(504) 568-3050	tydell.nealy@eeoc.gov
New York	Larry Pincus	(917) 816-6672	Lawrence.pincus@eeoc.gov
Norfolk	Herbert Brown	(757) 441-6669	Herbert.brown@eeoc.gov
Oakland	Joyce Hendy	(510) 637-3230	joyce.hendy@eeoc.gov
Oklahoma City	Edward Elizondo	(214) 655-3386	jim.habas@eeoc.gov

EEOC LIAISON OFFICE	CONTACT	TELEPHONE NUMBER	E-MAIL
Philadelphia	Edward McCaffrey	(215) 440-2671	edward.mccaffrey@ eeoc.gov
Phoenix	Krista Watson	(602) 640-4995	Krista.watson@ eeoc.gov
Raleigh	Richard Walz	(919) 856-4022	richard.walz@eeoc. gov
Richmond	Gloria Underwood	(804) 771-2141	gloria.underwood@ eeoc.gov
San Antonio	Yolanda Torres	(210) 281-7607	Yolanda.torres@ eeoc.gov
San Francisco	Michael Baldonado	(415) 356-5042	michael.baldonado @eeoc.gov
San Jose	Dee Cooper	(408) 291-7352	Dequese.cooper@ eeoc.gov
Seattle	Judi Cotner	(206) 220-6866	judith.cotner@eeoc. gov
St. Louis	Sharron Blalock	(314) 539-7937	Sharron.blalock@ eeoc.gov
Tampa	Manuel Zurita	(813) 228-2280	Manuel.zurita@ eeoc.gov
Washington, DC	Janice Proctor	(202) 523-3236	Janice.proctor@ eeoc.gov

GLOSSARY

Administrative Closure—Refers to a charge that is closed for administrative reasons, which may include (i) the failure to locate the charging party; (ii) the charging party failed to respond to EEOC communications; (iii) the charging party refused to accept full relief; (iv) the charging party requests withdrawal of a charge without receiving benefits or having resolved the issue; (v) there is no statutory jurisdiction. In addition, a charge may be closed due to the outcome of related litigation which establishes a precedent that makes further processing of the charge futile.

American Civil Liberties Union (ACLU)—A nationwide organization dedicated to the enforcement and preservation of rights and civil liberties guaranteed by the federal and state constitutions.

Americans with Disabilities Act (ADA)—A federal law which prohibits employers from discriminating on the basis of a "qualified" disability as set forth in the statute.

Back Pay—Wages awarded to an employee who was illegally discharged.

Base Rate Pay—An employee's basic hourly rate excluding overtime.

Blue-Collar Workers—Generally refers to individuals engaged in manual labor.

Bureau of Labor Statistics—A division of the U.S. Department of Labor that complies statistics related to employment.

Charge—Under Title VII, refers to a formal allegation filed with the EEOC by a charging party claiming to have been discriminated against by an employer, labor union or employment agency when applying for a job or on the job because of race, color, religion, sex, or national origin.

Equal Employment Opportunity Commission (EEOC)—Federal agency responsible for interpreting and enforcing the employment anti-discrimination provisions under federal law, including Title VII of the Civil Rights Act of 1964, as amended.

Employment Discrimination—Under Title VII, employment discrimination occurs when an employer denies an individual employment opportunities or otherwise affects their terms and conditions of employment based on race, color, religion, sex, or national origin.

FEPA—A state or local fair employment practices agency where many charges are first deferred for a specific time period for handling prior to being forwarded to the EEOC.

Hostile Work Environment—A working environment that both a reasonable person would find hostile or abusive, and one that the particular person who is the object of the harassment perceives to be hostile or abusive. Hostile work environment is determined by looking at all of the circumstances, including the frequency of the allegedly harassing conduct, its severity, whether it is physically threatening or humiliating, and whether it unreasonably interferes with an employee's work performance. In a sexual harassment claim, a hostile work environment is one in which the victim is subjected to unwelcome and severe or pervasive repeated sexual comments, innuendoes, touching, or other conduct of a sexual nature which creates an intimidating or offensive place for employees to work.

Independent Contractor—An individual who contracts to perform services for others without qualifying legally as an employee.

Investigation—Under Title VII, refers to an official inquiry by the EEOC to determine whether a charging party's allegations are supported by the available evidence.

Mediation—Mediation is an informal process in which a neutral third party—the mediator—assists the opposing parties in reaching a voluntary, negotiated resolution of the complaint.

Merit Resolution—A charge with an outcome favorable to the charging parties and/or a charge with meritorious allegations. A merit resolution may include negotiated settlements, withdrawals with benefits, successful conciliations, and unsuccessful conciliations.

Negotiated Settlement—Refers to charges that are settled with benefits to the charging party as warranted by evidence of record. In such cases, the EEOC is a party to the settlement agreement between the charging party and the respondent, who may be an employer, union, or other entity covered by EEOC-enforced statutes.

No Reasonable Cause—Refers to the EEOC's determination that there is "no reasonable cause" to believe that discrimination occurred based upon the evidence obtained in investigation. The charging party may request a review of a no-cause finding by EEOC Headquarters officials and may exercise the right to bring private court action.

Quid Pro Quo Harassment—Latin for "something for something." Quid pro quo harassment is a form of sexual harassment where a manager, supervisor or a person of authority gives or withholds a work-related benefit in exchange for sexual favors. Typically, the harasser requires sexual favors from the victim, either rewarding or punishing the victim in some way.

Reasonable Cause—Refers to the EEOC's determination of "reasonable cause" to believe that discrimination occurred based upon evidence obtained in investigation. Reasonable cause determinations are generally followed by efforts to conciliate the discriminatory issues which gave rise to the initial charge. Some reasonable cause findings are resolved through negotiated settlements, withdrawals with benefits, and other types of resolutions, which are not characterized as either successful or unsuccessful conciliations.

Reinstatement—Refers to the return of an employee to employment from which he or she was illegally dismissed.

Retaliation—Overt or covert acts of reprisal against an individual who makes a discrimination complaint, or who cooperates with a discrimination investigation or proceeding.

Severance Pay—Monies paid to a terminated employee.

Sexual Harassment—Any unwelcome sexual advance, request for sexual favors, or verbal, written or physical conduct of a sexual nature by a manager, supervisor or co-worker.

Successful Conciliation—Refers to a charge with reasonable cause determination that is closed after successful conciliation. Successful conciliation results in substantial relief to the charging party and all others adversely affected by the discrimination.

Temporary Employee—An employee who is hired to work on a short-term basis.

Termination—Refers to cessation of employment, e.g. by quitting or dismissal.

Title VII—Refers to Title VII of the Civil Rights Act of 1964, as amended, which prohibits discrimination in employment based on race, color, religion, sex or national origin.

Unsuccessful Conciliation—Refers to a charge with reasonable cause determination that is closed after efforts to conciliate the charge are unsuccessful.

Wages—Compensation paid to an employee.

Whistleblower—An employee who reports on violations of the law which occur in the workplace.

White Collar Workers—Generally refers to individuals engaged in office work.

Withdrawal with Benefits—Refers to a charge that is withdrawn by the charging party upon receipt of the desired benefits. The withdrawal may take place after a settlement or after the respondent grants the appropriate benefit to the charging party.

Workplace Harassment—Any unwelcome verbal, written or physical conduct that either denigrates or shows hostility or aversion towards a person on the basis of race, color, national origin, age, sex, religion, disability, marital status or pregnancy that: (1) has the purpose or effect of creating an intimidating, hostile or offensive work environment; (2) has the purpose or effect of unreasonably interfering with an employee's work performance; or (3) affects an employee's employment opportunities or compensation.

Wrongful Discharge—An unlawful dismissal of an employee.

Zone of Employment—The physical area in which injuries to an employee are covered by worker compensation laws.

BIBLIOGRAPHY AND ADDITIONAL READING

Black's Law Dictionary, Fifth Edition. St. Paul, MN: West Publishing Company, 1979.

Cornell Law School Legal Information Institute. (Date Visited: September 2002) <http://www.law.cornell.edu/>.

The Federal Labor Relations Authority (Date Visited: September 2002) <http://www.access.gpo.gov/flra/>.

The Office of Personnel Management (Date Visited: September 2002) <http://www.oopm.gov/>.

The Office of Special Counsel for Immigration Related Unfair Employment Practices (Date Visited: September 2002) <http://www.usdoj.gov/crt/osc/>.

The Merit Systems Protection Board (Date Visited: September 2002)<http;//www.mspb.gov/>.

UCLA Law School (Date Visited: September 2002) <http://www.law.ucla.edu/>.

The United States Equal Employment Opportunity Commission (Date Visited: September 2002) <http://www.eeoc.gov/>.

The United States Department of Justice (Date Visited: September 2002) <http://www.usdoj.gov/>.

The United States Department of Labor (Date Visited: September 2002) <http://www.usdol.gov/>.